001.4

WRITERS & RESEARCHERS

Books in the 'Writing' series

Other books for Writers

INTERVIEWING TECHNIQUES
for
WRITERS &
RESEARCHERS

Susan Dunne

A & C Black • London

First published 1995
A & C Black (Publishers) Limited
35 Bedford Row, London WC1R 4JH

ISBN 0-7136-4192-4

A CIP catalogue record for this book is available from the British Library.

Designed and typeset by Janet Watson
Printed in the United Kingdom by Biddles Ltd, Guildford, Surrey.

CONTENTS

INTRODUCTION

For most writers, other than those who write purely personal works of fiction which draw from the contents of their head, heart, navel or other part of the anatomy, writing involves going out in to the world to search for information. Whilst some of this information may be readily available in libraries, archives and other research centres, there are occasions when research can be best done through a live source – in other words the writer needs to interview.

Interviews are often regarded as belonging solely to the province of journalism (and indeed interviews are very often the life blood of articles) but many other kinds of writing can benefit from a good interview. Whether you are a journalist who wants to write a profile about a celebrity, an historical fiction writer trying to gain information from an historian about social customs during a particular period or a writer of contemporary fiction who needs to find out about a day in the life of a dustman to give authenticity to your story, you will need to interview. Other writers and researchers who can benefit from interviews include students writing a thesis about a live subject or drawing on the expertise of someone in their field, local historians gathering oral history of the locality, genealogists tracing family history and people who write for a hobby and who may want to submit an occasional piece about an interesting local resident for the parish magazine. Even if all you want to write about are historical monuments for your county magazine, you will find that your work can be improved and enlivened by a few interesting quotes and opinions from an expert, and taking a break from the confines of a library or archive to gain information from a live source can be pleasantly refreshing. If you would like to be able to approach people who can help your writing and maybe help further your writing career you will need to learn interviewing skills.

There are many benefits to be gained from interviewing. For journalists interviews provide an almost limitless source of ideas for articles. Interviews can breathe life into your writing through lively quotes, anecdotes, and human interest stories. Interviewees can provide unique expert information, eye witness accounts and the kind of authenticity which is not readily available from the printed page. A spin-off for the writer is that interviews bring human contact into what is often a fairly solitary occupation and can help you to form contacts with others who are interested in your field. For many writers, interviewing offers a privileged glimpse into the lives of other people whose lifestyles and experiences may be totally different from their own. In the course of interviewing you will meet many interesting people who will inspire, intrigue and endear themselves to you in the space of a short time. When you can interview you are adding valuable skills to your repertoire as a writer and researcher which can lead you in many different directions.

Often writers are in the unenviable position of having to find out by trial and error how best to go about interviewing. Many would-be writers fail to reach their full potential because they lack the confidence or just don't know how to go out and use live sources to help them in their work. If you are new to interviewing the process may seem to be shrouded in mystique or you may feel that interviewing is only undertaken by a certain kind of writer. Whilst it takes time and effort to become a good interviewer (and the only effective way to learn how to interview is to go out and practise on live subjects), the freelance writer who follows certain basic guidelines is just as capable of conducting an interview as a seasoned journalist writing for a daily paper.

In this book I have described and outlined the basic procedures of interviewing which should enable you to conduct a competent interview. Whatever the reason for your interview, the interviewing process is largely similar in most cases – you will need to arrange a market or project, arrange an interview, conduct the interview, write up the interview and send it off for publication (where appropriate). The book traces these stages step by step and offers advice on choosing the best recording methods, preparation before the interview and what to do if something goes wrong. No two interviews are the same and no book could hope to cover every eventuality which you might encounter in an interview situation but I hope this book will help you get started on what many writers regard as one of the most enjoyable and productive parts of researching. Successful interviewing is a privilege and a pleasure – enjoy it.

A NOTE FOR RESEARCHERS For the sake of simplicity, I have often used the generic term 'writer' to cover both writers and researchers. Whilst the majority of researchers are working towards a final written work, whether this is a thesis, a book or a research paper, some may be researching for their own pleasure and interest. Genealogists and local historians may fall into this category. Whilst all researchers will need to record and store their findings, not everyone will need or want to prepare them for publication. If this is the case, you may want to skip the sections relating to publication and select what is going to be useful to you in the course of your research.

1
SOME COMMON QUESTIONS ABOUT INTERVIEWING

What is an interview

A writer's interview involves asking a designated person (or persons) for information and opinions in a structured way and recording the answers appropriately for the intended publication. That is the basis of all interviews. For many people the word 'interview' can conjure up negative connotations of being put on the spot and made to answer questions under pressure. Whilst some types of writing (investigative journalism for instance) may involve putting some pressure on the interviewee to give the required information, the majority of interviews by writers tend to be polite affairs where the interviewee is the expert and the interviewer is the learner.

Are there different kinds of interviews?

Interviews can vary considerably in length, depth and subject matter and they may be held over the phone or take place face to face. The nature of the interview and the form it finally takes on paper will be largely determined by the kind of work you are doing. For more on types of interviews see the next chapter.

Do I have to approach each interview differently?

Yes and no. Yes, in so far as each individual is different and you will need to adapt your style of interviewing to accommodate each person as best you can. No, in so far as the basic procedure for interviewing remains largely the same regardless of whom you are interviewing. Your task, whether you are talking to a rock star, a local housewife or a managing director, is always going to be extracting and recording information and/or opinions for your writing or project.

What part does interviewing play in writing?

An interview is part of a writer's research process, not an end in itself. In practice you will probably find that the amount of time spent actually interviewing is relatively small compared with the amount of time spent on securing the interview, finding a market and writing up your work. Even if you are writing a profile for a magazine article based entirely around an interview, the interview itself will be only one of several steps needed to complete the article. Nonetheless, interviewing can play a vital part in the research of many writers and the benefits from a good interview can far outweigh the initial efforts involved in setting up the process and in writing it up afterwards.

What are the uses of interviewing to the writer?

Below are just a few reasons why you may want to use interviews in your writing:

- To draw on expert information or 'I don't know but I know a man who does'.
- To check information. Writers labour under the burden of needing to get their facts right. Giving wrong information is a source of irritation to both the reader and the editor. Drawing on live expert information is one way of helping to prevent mistakes.
- To gain credibility. No writer can know everything, even about the subject on which he/she purports to be an expert. Adding an opinion or quote from an expert to your piece is one of the best ways of giving your work credibility and of making it sound properly researched.
- To give you the opportunity to write about people you are interested in and whom you think are worth writing about.
- To breathe life into your work by injecting a human voice or opinion.
- To sell copy. For journalists in particular, interviews can provide an endless source of potential article material and, more importantly, editors tend to like interview pieces.

Who needs to interview?

For some kinds of writing interviewing is essential – interviewing is part of the stock in trade of journalists who are very often dealing with live issues about live people. The more stately freelance feature writers would be missing a substantial number of markets if they were unable to do the occasional interview based piece or even to contact live sources for information. Biographers, particularly those of live subjects, wouldn't get very far if they didn't actually go out and talk to the person they are trying to write about, or, in certain cases where the subject's co-operation is not given, to colleagues, friends, enemies and relatives of their subject. Biographers of dead subjects (even long-dead subjects) may need to call on the expertise of others if they are attempting to write a rounded life – what would a present day medical expert make of Napoleon's alleged fits, or Alexander Pope's curvature of the spine? Recently one biographer explored the possibility that Emily Brontë could have been an anorexic and there has been much interest in the possible influence of childhood sexual abuse on the writings of Virginia Woolf. In short, any writer whose work can be helped or improved by drawing on a live source of information or expertise needs to interview.

Can anyone interview?

There is a prevalent (and mistaken) belief that interviewing is only done by staff journalists. Unless you are by some misfortune unable to speak or listen there is no reason why you cannot interview. The basic requirement for interviewing is that you can ask a series of structured questions and accurately record the answers. If you can fulfil these criteria then you can interview. However, should you wish to develop into a hard-hitting pressure interviewer or want to dig out the dirt on people for a tabloid newspaper, you will also need to develop other 'skills' and a personality or persona to match. For the purpose of this book it will be assumed that you are mainly interested in acquiring a working knowledge of interviewing skills and how to interview.

With the possible exception of journalists, writers as a breed have a reputation for being introverted. Even if this is true, introversion need not in itself be an obstacle and in some ways it can be a positive advantage. Interviews are concerned with getting other people to talk about themselves, not with talking about yourself. All interviewers need is to master a number of simple techniques to be able to interview effectively. From here they may want to go on to develop technique into art but this is not compulsory.

Who is interviewed?

Anyone from the proverbial man in the street to a world expert is a possible interview subject. Whom you interview depends on your writing project. A piece on public opinion on extra marital affairs might draw on the results of a vox-pop conducted with strangers (see chapter 2 under *Types of interview*), whereas a piece on rare metals might necessitate a call to a university science department to talk to an expert. Sometimes it may be just as convenient to interview your partner or best friend, and at other times several transatlantic phone calls might find the right person for you. Interviewees can be roughly divided into two categories:

- The interviewees are of primary importance – usually because they (or what they have done – sometimes it's a matter of both) are special in some way. This category could include the rich, famous, infamous and talented but could also include the ordinary person in extraordinary circumstances.
- The interviewee has expert, inside or special information which you need for your writing. Press officers, agents and witnesses are all potential sources for this kind of interview.

How do I go about finding someone to interview?

Usually you will need to track down someone at their home or place of work, through an agent or through your own connections. The answer is to look in the obvious places and follow any leads. For more on tracking down interviewees see under chapter 5, *Getting the interview*.

How do you approach someone to interview them?

Write, telephone or approach them in person. For more on approaching interviewees see under chapter 5, *Getting the interview*.

Where do I conduct an interview?

Unless you are interviewing over the phone or are approaching strangers in the street for their opinion, you will usually need to arrange a convenient place where you can talk to the person. When people agree to be interviewed, they are doing you a favour by offering their time and expertise, so it is polite to try to arrange the interview at a place which is convenient for them. For more on arranging a place to meet see under chapter 5, *Getting the interview*.

How long is an interview?

This is 'a piece of string' question. Interviews can last from a few minutes on the phone or grabbed with someone on the way out of a room or, for people like biographers, interviews can take place over many months, even years and can last for several hours at a stretch. A face-to-face interview for a magazine article will usually last for about an hour but there are no fixed rules about this. The length of your interview will depend both on the amount of information you want to ask and the availability of the interviewee. To some extent the time the interview takes may also be influenced by how much the interviewee is willing or otherwise to talk. The length of the interview can be discussed at the time the interview appointment is made (see chapter 5).

How much do I need to know about the subject before doing the interview?

The answer is as much as possible. Research is an essential part of good interviewing – it will inform your questions and give you credibility in the eyes of the interviewee. For more on research see chapter 6, *Preparation before the interview*.

Are there any legal considerations I should know about before interviewing?

Yes. The most important one is libel. For more on libel see under chapter 11, *Transcribing and writing up*.

What sort of questions do you ask at an interview?

The questions you ask will be largely dictated by the market for which you are writing and the nature of work. Unless you are conducting a questionnaire or a vox-pop (see next chapter), the questions will be different every time. For more on asking questions see chapter 6, *Preparation before the interview* and chapter 8, *Conducting the interview.*

2
METHODS OF INTERVIEWING AND TYPES OF INTERVIEW

In this chapter I will give a brief overview of the most common methods of interviewing and types of interview and their uses to the writer. The method and type of interview you use will to a large extent be determined by the nature of the work you are doing. If you have a set writing project in mind you may have a very clear idea of whom you are going to interview and by what means (a profile of a local author for instance would almost certainly entail a face-to-face interview and would be most suitable for a feature in a magazine), but if you are intending to do a lot of interviewing you will probably find that certain types of interview are more appropriate for certain kinds of research or writing and the following looks at some of the options which are available to you. If you are a freelance journalist you will find that, the more kinds of interview you are able to do, the more markets will open up to you. Most writers find that they have a preference for one kind of interviewing over another – some may prefer going out to meet someone in person, whilst others may appreciate the more efficient, if less personal, method of telephoning an interviewee. Whatever your preferences, the kind of interview you do should ultimately be dictated by the nature of the work you are doing.

Face-to-face interviewing

If you are planning a full-length feature or intend to write extensively about someone, a face-to-face meeting is best, unless you are coming up to a deadline and the other person happens to be in the opposite hemisphere. In some ways this is the most satisfying way of conducting an interview because your interviewee has set aside a specific amount of time to see you and because you have the opportunity to delve deeper into your subject and gain more information than is usually the case in a telephone interview or in a few seconds which you manage to grab at the end of a meeting or press conference. In a face-to-face interview surroundings, body language, facial expression, and actions within a known environment can all provide potentially useful information for your work. Additionally there is more opportunity to build up a rapport with someone if you are sitting in a living room drinking coffee than if you are addressing an unknown face over the phone. Probably the principal drawback of setting up a face-to-face interview is that it involves time and often travel expenses. There are occasions when the location may be less than ideal for interviewing or there may be distractions of the dog, child, noise variety, but overall many interviewers find meeting someone in person the most interesting and enjoyable way of conducting an interview. For how to conduct a face to face interview see under chapter 8, *Conducting the interview.*

Telephone interviewing

It is unusual to interview subjects on the phone if you are intending to write about them in any detail and, if this is the case, you would be more likely to conduct a face-to-face interview. There are, however, several reasons why interviewing on the phone might be more appropriate than going out to see someone. If, for instance, your interviewee lives a long way off it might be more sensible in terms of saving time and travel costs to interview over the phone. If your interviewee is fairly important to your work but is important for expertise rather than personality (a psychiatrist specialising in the dynamics of dysfunctional families who may be able to help you with an article about what makes a good family for example), you will probably find that the kind of information he or she can offer can be obtained more efficiently over the phone than by a meeting. If you or your interviewee are particularly busy, about to leave the country or if a deadline is imminent, a telephone call can be a great time-saver. Staff feature writers who may need to conduct several interviews a week often do them over the phone just to save time.

If you have to decide between proposing to do a face-to-face interview or a telephone interview, you will need to weigh up some of the following pros and cons. One of the main advantages of telephone interviewing is that you can sometimes get immediate access to the person you wish to speak to there and then. You can also avoid wasting both time and a journey if the person you want to speak to turns out not to have the information you need, although this is something which will usually emerge at the setting-up stage. People who are especially busy may prefer to deal with the matter over the phone rather than set aside a valuable slot in their diary when they can meet you (which may be several weeks or months hence). The drawbacks of telephoning are that you have no access to a person's body language (although if you are only gathering factual information, this is not usually a problem) and it can be more difficult to set up a rapport with someone over the phone. It is also easier for someone to refuse to give you an interview over the phone by calling a halt to the conversation there and then: 'Sorry I've got to go'. Recording information over the phone is more difficult and, whilst it is probably overall more economical than travelling to an interview, it can and does run up your phone bill. For more on how to conduct a telephone interview see under chapter 8, *Conducting the interview.*

The written approach

Occasionally it may seem more appropriate to interview by written rather than verbal communication. If your subject lives a long way off and is difficult to get hold of either in person or over the phone you may find that your best approach is either through a letter or by sending a questionnaire. Written approaches tend to be used for more formal kinds of interview such as in academic and research circles. For more on the uses of a questionnaire or letter in interviewing, see below under *Types of interview*. If you require a lot of written information from your subjects or are aware that they are very busy, a tentative query letter or telephone call first, checking whether they are willing to help you, may seem appropriate.

Types of interview

Interviews, like interviewees, come in many shapes and sizes. Whilst the basic techniques of asking for and recording information will remain to a large extent the same whatever kind of interview you are doing, the type of interview you conduct will be determined by the nature and needs of your intended publication or use of the material. Some of the types of interviews outlined below will have a specific application for a specific type of writing. Profile articles are obviously the province of journalists but much the same methods can be used by other kinds of writers such as local historians. Similarly other kinds of interviews, such as interviewing an expert for their expertise, the vox-pop or the questionnaire, may be equally useful to anyone who needs to research information for their writing.

Interviewing for a profile article

Interview-based pieces tend to fulfil the popular image of a journalist's interview. Unlike a short news item where a journalist may interview someone for the sake of getting a good quote or revealing what the experts say, profile articles involve more leisurely in-depth interviewing where the writer may spend some time talking to a person in some detail. Face-to-face interviews are usually used for profile articles. In this kind of interview the focus is likely to be on the persons themselves either because of a particular achievement (a best-selling author for example) or because of something that has happened to them (a winner of the National Lottery) or sometimes simply because of an accident of birth (relation of the rich, famous or infamous).

Most Sunday supplements and most of the popular magazines will run at least one such interview per edition and some may run several. Typically, profile articles tend to run to at least 1000 words and some are considerably longer. There is often a high incidence of quotes in the piece and some may consist entirely of the words of the person being interviewed – articles describing 'A Day in the life of. . .' are typical – although it is usual for the entire piece to have been prompted by the skilful questioning and writing up by an interviewer (see chapter 11, *On writing up*).

Interview-based pieces often take a particular slant. A typical day in the life of the rich and famous might be one but other old chestnuts are the 'Triumph over tragedy' stories which often feature in popular women's magazines, and personal experience stories of the 'How I gave up my day job as a civil servant and became a geisha' kind. Local-interest publications may focus on local people because of their house, garden, job or travel experience. It is usually not sufficient to interview someone who is famous simply because of that fame and most magazines and papers, especially special-interest publications, require a particular angle that would make the piece appropriate for that publication. For more on finding an angle see chapter 4, *Choosing a market*.

For freelance journalists interview-based pieces are especially useful. Editors tend to like them because these kinds of articles provide new material and, if the interview subject is well known, the article can help boost sales. Moreover, it is often possible for freelancers to use the same interview for articles for several magazines or papers. So, in terms of time and cost effectiveness, this kind of interview can be particularly useful. For more on multiple marketing see chapter 12.

The popularity of this kind of article can be seen by glancing through a random selection of papers and magazines. A look at my weekly local paper reveals an interview with a lady on the dangers posed to horse riders by traffic; the monthly local magazine includes an interview with a local business man who has set up a cheese-manufacturing company; an interview with a local artist on the way she has decorated her home; and an interview with a local author on his latest book. This makes one third of the contents of the local magazine interview pieces. In one of the weekend national papers alone I find an article with a famous actress discussing the joys and miseries of single parenthood, a routine questionnaire with a well-known sportsman and a chef describing his favourite restaurant. As an exercise try glancing through your favourite magazine to see how many articles of this kind you can find. See if you can think of any other ideas for interviews for a particular publication – this could be either with someone famous or someone who is personally known to you and would seem an appropriate person to interview for that publication. Being able to do an interview-based article considerably opens up your market opportunities.

Articles involving several interviews

Some writing projects, especially those which explore a particular issue or aim to give a rounded picture, may necessitate several interviews to get a variety of opinions or viewpoints. A local historian writing about a rural community in the 1920s would obviously want to draw on as many live testimonies as possible from as many different walks and backgrounds to give a complete picture, and biographers in particular may draw on many interviews in the course of their research. Many articles can include interviews from several different sources and these tend to differ from the vox-pop-based articles (see below) in that they are usually more focused and interviewees are chosen carefully because they may have something of special interest to contribute to the contents of the article rather than simply for gathering random opinions. An article on the social lives of women who have high-powered jobs or men who gave up marriage for the priesthood might be examples of this kind of article. You would probably need a minimum of three interviewees to give a broad enough spectrum of experience and your primary task (apart from selling the idea to an editor) would be to find subjects who are suitable to be interviewed for the article. Whilst the nature of the publication you are writing for might require that you choose subjects in a particular age group or social class (for more on this see under chapter 4, *Choosing a market*) you should try, within these limits, to find a varied selection of interviewees. Choosing three or more women who all work for the same firm would probably not be very wise as this could give only a limited perspective.

You should also aim to be as broad minded in your approach as possible – it is unlikely that each interviewee will give the same answer or the same opinion to the questions you ask, and you may in fact find that there is some disagreement in the opinions and answers expressed. That's fine, because an article of this nature is likely to be discursive, but, if you have set out to prove a point (for instance that all women who earn a lot of money must find it difficult to find time for a social life), you may find yourself running into difficulties when none of your interviewees supports this hypothesis or one or more of them disagrees. This is an issue which you could consider at the conception stage of the article and it is better in this case to start off with a question to which you hope to find some answers in the article rather than an opinion which you want to have confirmed by what your interviewees say. In an article of this nature you would probably need to ask each subject broadly similar questions. For more on interviewing more than one person see chapter 9, *In the event of. . .*

Press conferences

A press conference is usually called when a company or organisation has a particular item to promote or when there is a large amount of press interest in a particular subject. If you have never been to a press conference you can get some idea of how they operate by watching news broadcasts on television. Typically in a press conference members of the press and interested parties gather to listen to a presentation or statement which will be followed by an open floor in which those present can ask questions. Press conferences are usually (but not always) democratic affairs where everyone is entitled to ask a question, although a drawback can be that some people tend to hog the floor. Questions are either put through a mediator or they can be addressed directly to a particular person. Press conferences can consist of a panel of people or be mainly focused on one person such as a well-known playwright promoting his/her latest play at the local theatre.

It is sensible to have some idea of the kind of question you would like to ask beforehand (the kind of question you ask will usually be dictated by the demands of your publication). You are not, of course, limited to using only the answer to the question you ask for your final written piece and you may find that questions asked by others and the answers given yield useful copy, although, strictly speaking, you should not, when writing up, make yourself the interrogator if you haven't asked the question. Magazines and newspapers often receive invitations to press conferences but, if you are a freelance, you could contact the personnel offices of any organisation you are particularly interested in and ask to be kept informed of any forthcoming publicity events. Alternatively, if you have built up a working relationship with an editor, you could offer to go to press conferences, public meetings and publicity events on his behalf. Publications with a small editorial staff might be more than happy to send you.

The vox-pop

The term means voice of the people (*vox populi*, strictly speaking) and a vox-pop interview is one in which the interviewer gathers opinions from members of the public. This kind of interviewing is often useful for consumer articles, for light humorous articles (e.g. 'What do you buy for your most hated relative at Christmas?') and for doing surveys on the extent of public information and opinion about a particular issue (e.g. 'Have you heard of the new plans to ban fishing in the North Sea and what do you think about it?'). In some ways this can be the most daunting kind of interview as it means approaching total strangers without any pre arrangement. None the less, the vox-pop can be a very fruitful source of information, quotation and copy. Most vox-pop interviews are carried out in the street or in a shopping centre. Whom you decide to approach will depend on what you are writing about. A piece about health care in old age will probably lead you to target people who look as if they are of retirement age, whereas a piece on young unemployed people would obviously lead you to look for a younger age group. Generally, it is best to approach people who do not seem to be in an excessive hurry or are not weighed down with shopping bags. People sitting on benches are usually a good bet, as are single people. It is often a good idea to have an introductory patter worked out beforehand (try not to let it sound too mechanical) in which you briefly explain who you are, what you are interviewing for and what you want to ask questions about. Then ask something like 'Would you mind answering a few questions on what you think of the rise in VAT/council tax/cigarette prices?'. How many people you decide to ask will depend on the size of the piece, how much information you need and how broad a spectrum of opinions you require, but you should try to keep your questions quite short as you are imposing on someone's time – sometimes one or two questions is sufficient for this kind of interview. If the person says no just thank them and find someone else. Don't let it knock your confidence – some people simply don't like being asked questions – but in practice most people quite like to be asked for their opinion, in particular if they feel quite strongly about the issue you are raising.

Catching the moment (or interviewing on the hoof)

Occasionally you may meet someone whom you want to interview there and then. This kind of interview is frequently seen on television news broadcasts where the journalist tries to grab a few words from an important figure who is often midway between the car and the front door. Interviews of this nature are not for the reticent but they are potentially very useful. If you can catch someone in this manner, be sure of what you want to ask and have your question ready framed. Say who you are and what your publication is or why you need to ask the questions. Hold your tape recorder, if you are using one, as close to the subject as is reasonably polite. Do not try to detain people for long – most people won't mind answering the odd question in passing but, if they are hurrying to be somewhere else, your questions could be very irritating. NOTE: make sure you know the distinction between invading someone's private space and interviewing someone whilst officially on the job (see also chapter 5, *Getting the interview*).

Long-term interviewing

Whilst most interviews are one-off events where you enter briefly into someone else's life, some kinds of writing (particularly biography) may require that you hold lengthy interviews with one individual over a period of time. Many of the usual approaches to interviewing will apply – you will still need to arrange interview times and do your research beforehand but you will also need to be aware of and considerate about the level of commitment, time and stamina you are asking of your interviewee.

Questionnaire or letter?

Questionnaires are particularly useful where you require specific answers to fairly straightforward questions. Questionnaires can be conducted orally or by post. The major disadvantage of sending a questionnaire by post is that you may never get a reply. If you are sending a written questionnaire, include a covering business like letter explaining who you are and why you are writing and always enclose a stamped addresssed envelope (SAE). Questionnaires needing written replies should be typed on one side of A4 paper, leaving sufficient space for answers between questions. Questions should be concise and clear and it is a good idea to leave a space for any additional comments your interviewee may want to make. If you require only a small amount of straightforward information, a short letter might be a better way to approach your subject than a questionnaire and this is a matter for your own judgement. As with a questionnaire enclose an SAE. You will endear yourself and future interviewers to your interviewee if you send a postcard thanking them for their reply when you receive it. If you are conducting a questionnaire orally, the procedure is much the same as for a vox pop although you may have more specific interview subjects in mind for a questionnaire (see under chapter 5, for ways of tracking people down).

Getting a quote

This is not strictly an interview but can be useful for times when you need to add an expert opinion or quote to what you are writing. If for example you were doing an article or news piece about a recent increase in medical prescription charges and the effect this will have on people on a low income, you will probably concentrate your main interviewing on people who fit this category. However you may also like to get an official opinion from a relevant professional body. In the case given you could telephone the press officer of an organisation such as the British Medical Association (BMA) to ask how they react to the news. In this case you may only want to ask this question but you will need to have your question and means of recording the answer ready prepared. See also *Telephone interviewing*, chapter 8).

3
TOOLS FOR THE JOB

Methods of recording

All the material which arises in the course of an interview should be recorded for possible future use and the kind of interview you do will probably dictate the best method of recording your information. It would be unwise, for example, to do a two-hour in-depth interview from which you hope to be able to write several thousand words by relying solely on memory. Equally, if you want to do a ten-minute interview to check some basic facts, a tape recorder might seem rather excessive. How you choose to record an interview is largely a matter of personal discretion, although there is always the possibility of factors beyond your control influencing the choice – if someone insists that you do an interview in a swimming pool, neither a notepad nor a tape recorder would be much use. Fortunately instances like this are rare and you can usually predict which method will work on the day.

In this chapter I will assess the merits and drawbacks of various tools and methods for recording an interview and will then consider other equipment which is potentially useful for anyone who wants to interview on a regular basis. The basic materials needed for interviewing are very simple and for your purposes you may need nothing more than the interviewer's stock-in-trade of a notepad and pen. However, the advances of technology have affected interviewing as much as everything else and many writers now use tape recorders and elaborate word-processing packages as a matter of course. If you do not have access to the materials outlined below, don't feel obliged to go out and buy them all at once or feel that you cannot start interviewing until you have bought a state-of-the-art tape recorder and designer business cards. A colleague of mine started interviewing from a houseboat which had neither a telephone, electricity nor a proper postal address – it didn't stop him from setting up and writing some excellent interviews.

Recording information

When you interview you need a means of recording information quickly, efficiently and accurately. Unfortunately for interviewers the speaking voice is considerably faster than the writing hand. This is a problem which all interviewers have to overcome and to do this you have to devise a method of recording that works best for you, but you also need to take into account the needs of the interviewee – not being able to get the information down quickly enough can disrupt the flow of the interview, whilst some interviewees may balk at the thought of speaking into a tape recorder. No method is one-hundred-per-cent foolproof and experience will tell you what will be most useful to you for conducting your interviews. Below is an assessment of the merits and drawbacks of the principal methods of recording information.

Notepad and pen

This is very much the brass-tacks approach to interviewing and the notepad and pen have traditionally been the tried and trusted tools of journalists. Most notepads are suitable for recording (although one covered in cartoon characters may not create the best impression at a strictly formal interview). Probably the most useful kind is the spiral bound notepad available from newsagents which you can keep on your lap and whose pages can be easily flipped over. Expensive designer pens are not necessary for interviewing – fountain or cartridge pens can run out of ink or blot at awkward moments so opt for whatever is most simple and most reliable. An ordinary ballpoint pen will do the job just as well, although you should take a spare one for back up.

Taking notes

If you choose to record your information by pen you are then faced with the problem of how to write the information down quickly enough. It is very difficult, and perhaps impossible, to record people speaking at a normal speed without having to ask them to pause or repeat themselves at frequent intervals. Whilst your interviewee probably won't mind obliging you once or twice, repetition and pauses can become tedious and can eat into inter-viewing time that could probably be better spent asking more questions. As you will not be able to get everything down in longhand, taking notes is one possible solution. If you are in the habit of extrapolating important pieces of information from what someone says, you may find it relatively easy to record your interview in this way, but, if you are not, an interview is not the place to start practising. No matter how good your note-taking is, you will probably still miss out on large sections of what is said but this may not always be a problem. In many interviews you may be more concerned about getting down the factual content of the interview rather than getting a large number of quotes and in this case taking notes may be quite adequate. You can invent your own method of taking notes – using phonetic spelling, missing out vowels and using abbreviations can speed things up considerably. 'C wt u cn cum up wiv.'

Shorthand

An alternative to taking notes is to record your information in shorthand but, unless you are already a shorthand secretary or have made use of short-hand in the recent past, you will need to have built up fairly high speeds before relying on shorthand in an interview situation. Journalists are still taught shorthand because on some occasions using a tape recorder is not possible – tape recorders cannot be taken into law courts, for example, and in some locations tape recording can be very difficult. If you are intending to do a lot of interviewing a course of shorthand may be worth considering. Teeline is the shorthand that young jounalists are encouraged to learn and shorthand courses are often available through evening classes, at adult education centres and through local colleges of further education. If you cannot attend a course, it is perfectly feasible to teach yourself and there are a number of books available such as *Teeline Shorthand* in the 'Made Simple' series which is aimed as much at the self-taught student as at the student attending a class. The other major school of shorthand is the Pitman school which offers both New Era which is particularly fast (speeds can reach as high as 200 words a minute) and Pitman 2000. In learning shorthand you should be able to double or triple your writing speeds but the disadvantage of shorthand is that, unless you use it regularly, writing speeds drop off fairly quickly.

You can get some idea of what it is like to record an interview in short-hand or by using notes by practising on a radio or television interview for a short time. Doing this will give you some practice of what to expect in a real live interview situation. Frequent practice should improve your recording speeds considerably.

Advantages of using a notepad and pen Perhaps one of the biggest attractions of using a pen and pad is that interviewees are not usually intimidated by a harmless note book and a ballpoint pen in the same way that they might be by a tape recorder. Similarly, if you as the interviewer are new to interviewing, using a notepad and pen does not feel quite so formal as using a tape recorder and some people can find it helpful to have something to do with their hands during an interview as well as having something on which to focus. As you will also be writing your interview questions in the notepad, you will be able to record each answer under the relevant question which can save time in unravelling it all after the interview. Additionally, unless you drop your notepad in a river or accidentally leave it behind on a bus, the information you have recorded is fairly safely contained within its covers.

Disadvantages of using a notepad and pen There are several reasons why recording the interview information on paper can be less than satisfactory. One of the main ones is that, in your effort to get the information down, you may find that you are unable to give enough attention to the interviewee. Writing down information involves frequent loss of eye contact and whilst this might work to your advantage with a very nervous interviewee other people may find it irritating or even offensive and it can be perceived as lack of interest on your part (see also under *Body language* in chapter 8, *Conducting the interview*). A rather more serious drawback is that in the event of a libel charge you do not have the hard and fast evidence of taped material to draw on (see also chapter 11, *Transcribing and writing up*, on libel). And, as previously mentioned, the slowness of recording by hand will necessarily mean that you will have to sacrifice some of your material because you cannot get it down quickly enough. Another problem with writing down information is that interviewees will very rarely give you all the information you need in the order for which you ask for it and there will necessarily be some ranging backwards and forwards from one point to another. The result can be a rather scrappy mess of information in your notebook which you will have to disentangle when you get home.

Whilst notepads are compact and portable, you may find that the circumstances of an interview can sometimes make it difficult to write down the information satisfactorily. If someone insists on taking a dog for a walk across the moors whilst they give you an interview or suggests that you do it in a jacuzzi, you may find yourself rather constrained. Under these circumstances it is probably better to explain your difficulty and ask whether the interview can be done sitting down afterwards. Going for a walk with someone beforehand may be fairly beneficial as it will give you the chance to break the ice and may provide some useful facts for your piece.

Memory

Although it is fairly unusual to rely purely on memory to record the stuff of interviews, there may be some when you feel this to be most appropriate or even some when you have no choice but to grab the moment and ask your questions there and then without access to a notepad or tape recorder. Few people are lucky enough to have total recall but holding on to important information for the short term is feasible, especially if the interview is relatively short. As long as you make an indelible record of the contents of the interview at the earliest opportunity, you should be able to rely on memory from time to time.

Advantages of memory

The beauty of simply storing information in your head is that you do not have to worry about the limitations of writing it down which can seem too slow or too much of a distraction from the interview itself. Nor do you have to worry about the technical and atmospheric drawbacks of the tape recorder (see below). You can give your interviewee your full attention and, if the interview is fairly short, you can record your information as verbatim as possible at the first opportunity.

Disadvantages of memory

The obvious drawback of relying solely on memory for interviews is that you may forget what was said. You may also be in danger of rewriting what was said because you cannot remember the exact words. Whilst this may not be too much of a hindrance most of the time (after all, it is unlikely that your interviewee will remember exactly what has been said either), there is always the danger of getting it seriously wrong or saying something libellous. The longer the time lapse between the interview and the time when you can commit the contents of your memory to paper, the greater the room for error, so, if you do have to rely on this method, writing up the interview contents should be a priority. If you envisage having to do interviews on the spur of the moment, it is a good idea to carry a notepad or recorder around with you at all times. Relying on memory for full-length and face-to-face interviews should only be done in exceptional circumstances. The biographer Deirdre Bair was forced to rely entirely on this method when writing the biography of Samuel Beckett who forbade her to use any method of recording in his presence. The result is still an excellent biography.

Tape recorders

Nowadays the tape recorder is an inherent part of many interviewers' equipment and most interviewers will agree that the tape recorder is a wonderful invention with many advantages and a few disadvantages. If you choose to use a tape recorder it should intrude as little as possible – opting for your teenage child's ghetto-blaster is unlikely to create a good impression. Whilst you can use the slightly old-fashioned square black recorders with the external microphone, probably the best type of recorder is the pocket-sized recorder or dictation machine which contains its own microphone and is commonly available from most electrical goods shops. Prices vary but, if interviewing is likely to be an important or frequent part of your writing and researching life, it is advisable to buy the best kind of tape recorder that you can afford. Prices vary from about twenty to several hundred pounds and models are available at high-street electrical goods shops and some office stationery shops. Some machines have a device whereby they can be operated by a foot pedal which means that you can have both hands free for typing when you come to transcribe the tape. Bear in mind that tape recorders are fairly delicate machines which do not take kindly to being dropped and, if there are any signs of a problem with your machine prior to an interview, you will need to find an appropriate substitute. It is good practice always to carry a notepad and pen in case for some reason you cannot use your tape recorder or the machine breaks down. Some tape recorders are voice activated which means that, if there is a silence in the conversation, they will cease to record. It is best to avoid using this kind of recorder for an interview as it may cease to pick up simply because someone is talking quietly, is on the other side of the room or has just paused for breath. When a voice-activated tape recorder has stopped, it requires the sound of a voice to set it in motion again and you may find that parts of what someone has said are missing because the tape has not begun to record as soon as the voice starts again. Another drawback of the voice-activated tape is that it is apt to be a great cause of anxiety to the interviewer who is conscious of it stopping and fears that its may not start again.

As well as the tape recorder you will need to ensure that you have a supply of good batteries for every interview. Some interviewers insist on using new batteries for every interview they do and there is something to be said for this seeming excessive caution. If your battery runs out mid tape you may not notice and you could arrive home with half a tape missing or an incomprehensible tape. Perhaps more importantly, the knowledge that you have new batteries in your recorder gives you the peace of mind to let the tape run without having to constantly worry about checking it, thus taking your attention away from the interview itself. You should give your tape recorder a trial run beforehand to make sure that the batteries are working (dud new batteries are not unknown) and it is often a good idea to carry spares just in case.

When using a tape for an interview it should be completely blank and you should label it beforehand (or at least immediately after) with the contents and the date (e.g. Interview Mr Davis, Browncester Museum 13.5.95) for easy future reference. The most common kind of tape is the 60-minute one (i.e. 30 minutes on each side) or the 90-minute one (45 minutes on each side). Unless you are doing a very short interview, you will probably need to turn the tape over in the middle of an interview and you may find that you lose some of what your interviewee is saying as a result, but this is usually unavoidable. When you have used a tape for an interview, do not record over it again because in the unlikely event of libel it may be required as evidence (see chapter 11, *Transcribing and writing up*).

Advantages of tape recording

The obvious advantage of a tape recorder is that under normal circumstances it records everything with total accuracy and requires a minimum of effort on your part (basically switching the recorder on at the beginning, turning it over and then off at the end). The recorder leaves you free to give your interviewee your total attention, to take notice of your surroundings and not to have to worry about whether you have got something down accurately or not. Furthermore, tape recorders can catch nuances in tone which are lost on notepads and they can be a very helpful aid for helping you recall your interviewee and the circumstances of the interview. With a tape recorder you can play back the interview as many times as necessary to extract the information you need from it. Tape recorders can give a professional feel to the whole proceeding (ghetto-blasters excepted) and can help to create your image as a professional person who takes what they are doing seriously.

Disadvantages of tape recording

Occasions when a notepad and pen outweigh a tape recorder are rare but there are times when it is just simpler to take things down by hand. A few people really do not feel comfortable when talking into a tape recorder and may become more concerned about the sound of their own voice on tape. Because of its professional appearance a tape recorder can be intimidating, in particular to 'ordinary people' who are not normally the subject of interviews. Whilst the opposite could happen – some people feel very important talking into a tape recorder – you may find that your interviewees are less likely to be themselves if they know that they are on tape. The result can be a change in accent, style and presentation of information and a very uncomfortable interviewee. Deciding when to use a tape recorder or not with someone who appears uncomfortable is a matter for your judgement. Most people can overcome their initial distaste and can ignore the presence of the tape recorder altogether when they become increasingly involved in the interview, but for some the presence of a tiny machine on the table may cause them to clam up completely. Perhaps the best option is to be prepared to switch to a notepad and pen (or even memory) if you feel the presence of the tape recorder will ultimately do more harm than good (see also chapter 8, *Conducting the interview*).

As well as the possible discomfort of the interviewee, you will need to overcome any discomfort you may have initially about using a tape recorder. Many people who are new to interviewing can feel slightly fraudulent when producing a brand-new tape recorder which they have never used before, because they may have a sneaking feeling that they are not really professional enough to use it. There are two possible ways around this – the first is to practise beforehand on a friendly guinea pig until you feel happy about using a tape recorder in a formal interview situation (it's also a good idea to experience being interviewed on tape yourself so that you have some idea of the effects it may have on your interviewee). The second is to simply come clean with your interviewee and say 'I'm not used to this, it's a new one' (you probably won't gain anything by also adding that you are completely new to interviewing and have never done it before so perhaps silence would be the better policy on that score). As your interviewee will probably be fairly nervous anyway, they may appreciate the fact that you are feeling a certain amount of discomfort too and this can be an ice-breaker, especially if you make a joke out of it where appropriate. Finally, remember to take the price tag off.

In order to get the best out of your interview it is often helpful to transcribe the contents of the tape on to paper. Whilst it is not always necessary to transcribe everything, most people find writing down the tape contents before getting down to the piece itself rather tedious. There is no real way around this, except to keep playing the tape backwards and forwards as you are writing your piece, but this can be equally tedious and you stand a chance of missing out something useful from the tape. On the whole you have to accept that this is not the most stimulating part of interviewing but it does help you get a clear idea of the interview contents and I sometimes think of transcribing as the cost I pay for having everything perfectly recorded for me. I don't think it's too high a price to pay.

Tape recorders are as subject to Murphy's Law as any other piece of technology. If a tape recorder can go wrong it will and it is very easy to wipe out a tape's contents at the push of a button. Treat recorded tapes with great care. Whilst you can sometimes avoid having a tape break down in the middle of an interview if you check it beforehand, there are never any guarantees that this won't happen. For details on what to do if a tape recorder fails to work in an interview see chapter 9, *Trouble shooting*. On the whole, if you have bought a good piece of equipment which is guaranteed you should not have to face this most annoying problem but Murphy's Law is not subject to 'shoulds' and 'oughts'.

Whilst tape recorders are fine for recording within the confines of an office or a quiet drawing room, not all interviews take place in a totally convenient environment. As pointed out previously, interviews can take place in the oddest of locations – holding on to a tape recorder or trying to thrust a microphone towards your interviewee whilst clinging to the sides of a mountain or suspended from a bungee rope is less than ideal. If you can foresee this problem, it may be possible to avoid it by suggesting that you tape record the interview before or after doing anything more exciting. Another factor to bear in mind when doing a taped interview is the possibility of background noise interference. With more primitive types of recording machines this could cause quite a problem. Present-day dictation machines tend to be more sophisticated and can absorb both background noise and the voices of the nearest speakers but, if you have any doubts, try doing a trial run in a noisy environment to see how much noise your tape picks up and whether your own voice is still audible above it. At the same time you could test what the range of sound pick up is. Thrusting a tape recorder or microphone into the mouth or up the nostrils of an interviewee tends to be more the province of television journalists trying to catch as much of what someone says as possible before they are whisked off elsewhere. For most interviewers, the tape recorder is placed equidistant between the two parties and it's a good idea to check when you purchase the machine what distances can be picked up.

If you are a struggling freelance writer, it is quite likely that you are also struggling financially. When things are really tight (and this is something most freelance writers have to deal with at some point), the cost of a new machine, batteries and tapes might seem like yet another drain on scant resources. If this is the case, stick with the notepad and pen until you can (if you want) afford a tape recorder, and remember that there was a time when everyone was dependent on taking interviews down manually. If you are operating a business as a freelance writer you may be able to claim back the costs of recording machines and accessories such as batteries and tapes as a tax rebate. Hang on to all relevant receipts however small they may seem.

One final drawback of tape recorders is that you are obliged to listen to yourself on tape. Disliking the sound of your own voice on tape is a seemingly universal phenomenon but there is no getting round it.

Whilst this may seem like a long list of possible drawbacks, the overall advantages of a tape recorder far outweigh the disadvantages and most interviewers would not leave home without one. They are particularly good for long interviews where gathering a lot of quotes and information is necessary.

Other tools for interviewing
Telephone
Most interviews are arranged over the phone and therefore you should have access to one, if not at home then at least at work. Payphones can create a rather less than professional impression particularly if your money or phone card runs out and some of them tend to emit a rather annoying bleep. Sometimes it is important that your interviewee is also able to contact you – they may want to ring you back to arrange an interview time, to confirm one or to alter one – so if you do not have access to a phone of your own try to arrange it so that messages can be left with someone who has got one. You may occasionally need to arrange an interview over a pay phone because you are only able to contact your interviewee at a time when you are out on the road. If this is the case make sure you have plenty of change, an unused phonecard or a BT chargecard (unless, that is, you have a mobile phone). Some public telephones will now accept major credit cards.

Camera

Many publications will have their own staff photographer but the more impoverished (or possibly just cheapskate) ones may expect you to take a picture as well as write your piece. For interviews you may be expected to produce a photograph of the interviewee and/or something related to the interview (see under chapter 8, *Conducting the interview*, for taking photos). If you are expecting to take a number of photos in connection with your writing career, it will probably be worth your while to invest in a fairly good camera. Whilst you may not always be paid for the picture, photographs can often attract a fee which may be as much as your written piece (and sometimes considerably more), so you need to choose your camera carefully. You can get the best advice on this from professional camera shops or, not quite such good advice, from electrical retail shops which sell cameras amongst other things. Whether you take photos in black and white or colour will depend on the needs of your publication. Most publications prefer colour photographs to be transparencies but it is advisable to check this beforehand. If you are a freelance journalist hoping to sell stories about your interview to several markets, it is often a good idea to take both black-and-white and colour photos to increase your potential markets. Usually this is best done by taking two cameras along for the interview, but this does mean either having two in your possession or having access to another one which you can borrow. As with tape recorders you should make sure that you are using fairly new batteries which have not been left in the machine for any appreciable period of time and remember to take a flash if this is a detachable part of your machine. Buy professional-quality film that is the right speed for your camera and the lighting conditions you anticipate.

Contact book

Many writers and most journalists carry a contact book around with them. For journalists actively involved in networking this is an essential part of their equipment. If you are doing a number of interviews or expect to do a number in the future, a contact book is a very useful way of keeping hold of addresses and phone numbers of your interviewees. Whilst this can also be done by simply incorporating names into your normal address book, it both feels and is more professional and better organised to keep interviewee details separate. A contact book is a ready source of personal reference which does away with the need for scraps of paper which are easily lost or filed in forgotten places or even inadvertently put in the waste-paper bin. Often a contact book can be just an address book reserved for interviewees and this has the advantage of listing names alphabetically. You should be able to find an appropriate book at most stationary shops.

Diary

A separate diary for recording times, dates and places of interview is not strictly necessary but it will help you to keep a clear picture of where and when you should be in a particular place. In this way you can avoid losing interview appointments with captains of industry *et al.* amongst hairdresser, dentist and dinner-party appointments. If you write a lot of articles or are engaged on a long-term project such as a biography or a thesis, it is often helpful to keep a separate work diary where, as well as interview dates, you can record deadlines and any other information that is of practical use to the completion of your project such as setting aside blocks of time for researching in the library.

Business cards

Again, business cards are not strictly necessary but some people like to use them and they are a very convenient way of passing on your details – for instance, when you leave an interview. Sometimes an interviewee may want to contact you afterwards with more information and handing out a business card is as good a way as any of passing on your details. Personal business cards can be made at most printers and you can add your own design – preferably something relevant and professional looking. A quill and ink pot or a typewriter would probably be more appropriate than a pink teddy bear.

Filing system

Some writers seem to thrive on the chaos created by mounds of paper but most find that organising their material can make the writing task much easier. How you organise your work is a personal matter but compartmen-talising the various components is often very useful and filing your work under separate headings in either a filing cabinet, filing case, or folder can prevent moments of temporary insanity when you are convinced that a vital piece of information is missing. Some people go in for elaborate colour-coding systems and catalogue their book shelves according to the files resting on them. If you find doing any of this helpful, do so too but, if you feel happy simply knowing in your head where things are, don't feel obliged to become hyper organised – being organised does not, after all, write your piece. As regards interview material, keep interview tapes separate from your Beatles/Beethoven/Black Sabbath tapes. You do not need to invest in a separate cassette holder for this purpose and a shoe box earmarked and felt-tip marked for the purpose will do equally well. If you have recorded your interview in a notebook you can keep it in an appropriate file.

Typewriters and word-processors

An apocryphal story tells how an elderly lady submitted a piece of writing to the radio which was hand written on lavatory paper. The radio editor was about to throw it in the bin when curiosity overcame him and he decided to read it. The piece happened to be very good and was subsequently bought and broadcast, but no writer, no matter how gifted, can avoid typing their work or having it typed for them now.

It is essential for writers who hope to publish their work or for researchers who need to present their work formally as in a thesis to type their work. You should therefore have access to a typewriter or word-processor or at least to someone who can type it for you. Writers wanting to do interviews will also need to send typewritten letters to interviewees occasionally. Hand-written letters are feasible but do not create a very professional impression, particularly if your handwriting isn't very good. It is nearly always better to type or word-process your work yourself – not only do you save on the cost of hiring someone else to do it, but even the most polished and seemingly complete piece of work may need a few last minute alterations. If you are new to the idea of typing up your work for publication, you could take a course in typing skills or, even better, word-processing skills. These are widely available through evening classes and, if you can't make it to an evening class there are many books available for the self-taught student. You can also teach yourself keyboarding skills on the word-processor and there are a number of manuals, teach-yourself books and computer tutorial programmes which can be obtained from most high-street stationery shops.

The word-processor has transformed the life of writers by taking the drudgery out of the physical process of committing words to paper. For interviewers word-processing can be particularly helpful because of the ease with which text can be altered and moved. When you come to write up your interview you may find that you need to do a substantial amount of reordering of your material. Whilst you can write an initial draft copy in longhand, it is much quicker and much more convenient if you can type directly on to the word-processor where text can easily be moved around at a later date. Another advantage of word-processing for the interviewer is that if you transcribe your tape (see chapter 11, *Transcribing and writing up*) directly on to a word-processor, you can simply move text around to fit in to your finished piece without having to write it out again.

4
CHOOSING AN INTERVIEWEE AND FINDING A MARKET

Deciding whom to interview

For some writers and researchers interviewing is so integral to their project that it is quite obvious whom they will need to interview. If you are writing a biography about a live subject, a thesis about a contemporary artist, a critical work on a living author or are discovering your genealogy, possible persons for interview will probably suggest themselves to you immediately. In some instances you may not know exactly whom you need to interview, but you may have a fairly clear idea of what kind of person will be useful to talk to, and this will usually be someone who has some expertise in the subject about which you are writing. If you are only intending to interview one person your task is greatly simplified, but many kinds of writing and research can benefit from drawing on a number of interviews to give a more rounded picture and this is something you will need to think about carefully before you begin to approach anyone. You may in the course of interviewing find that you need to refine your choice of subjects slightly or decide to interview a broader or narrower spectrum of people than you had originally intended, and this is perfectly in keeping with the nature of research – after all if you knew all the answers before you started out you would not be doing the research in the first place. As an example, a local history project on people's wartime experience in a particular factory contains its own choice of interview subjects but questions which you may need to consider include whether you are going to restrict your choice of interviews to factory floor workers, are you going to include employers too or are you going to specialise in women war workers? In some respects you may feel that you are taking a leap of faith as you may not yet know of or about every person you wish to interview when you start the undertaking, but again this is normal for many kinds of research. In the course of your writing and research you will probably find that one interviewee will lead you to seek out another as more and more information and sources become apparent to you. Often interviewees themselves can put you in touch with other potential subjects to talk to so that the whole process snowballs. For contacting interviewees see the next chapter.

Choosing an interview subject for journalists

Journalists, in particular freelance journalists who have to generate their own markets, differ somewhat from other writers in that they tend to be more opportunist about whom they interview. Freelancers are constantly on the look out for new interview subjects who may be the source of possible articles.

Journalists tend to choose interview subjects for one of the following reasons:

- The choice is suggested by the nature of the publication you write for or would like to write for. For instance, if you would like to write for a gardening magazine which regularly has a profile on gardeners and their gardens, you may go out and search for someone in your area who you think would be an appropriate choice of subject for the magazine. Similarly, you may know of a magazine which has a regular feature on people doing unusual jobs. You may want to approach the magazine with an idea about doing a feature on a lion tamer in your local circus, even if you do not yet know the lion tamer in person. You have therefore chosen your subject on the basis of the needs of the magazine.

- The choice is suggested by someone you know either in person or someone you know about. For instance, if you know someone who has battled against a serious illness and overcome it in a spectacular way, you may want to write about them for a 'True story' or 'Triumph over tragedy' type of feature. Alternately maybe there is an artist living in your street who you feel would be a good subject for an interview, or perhaps your friends have just returned from a spectacular travel adventure and you feel that their adventures would make a good feature article. In these cases the people themselves give you the idea for a piece and you think of the possible market (or markets) second.

In some cases your choice of interview may be decided on by both the above considerations. As you build up your contacts within the newspaper and magazine industry you will find that you become increasingly attuned to potential markets and potential interviewees. You will begin to recognize a possible story for an article immediately and you will have a number of ready-made markets to write for. When you reach this happy position you can spend less time researching the market before approaching editors and interviewees, and more time interviewing and writing.

When you have begun to become known as a journalist you may occasionally find that people come to you asking you to write a piece about them. This will often be someone who has something to promote or who wishes to publicise an event. In-house staff of magazines are often approached in this way, but there is no reason why freelance journalists should not also benefit from a interviewee who is offering themself to you. If you are very fortunate, you may be approached by editors asking you to do an article for their publication – if this involves interviewing they will often suggest which potential interviewees to approach.

Before finding a market

Whoever it is you decide to interview, it is important that you think your idea through carefully and do some proper market research before approaching either the interviewee or the eventual publisher. You will need to consider what angle you intend to take, which publication and readership you intend to write for and the form your writing will take.

You are not expected to know everything about your subject when you are in the initial stages of writing or researching, but you do need to know enough to convince the intended editor that you are sufficiently well informed to be taken seriously. At this stage bare bones information may suffice enough to demonstrate that you have a serious interest in the subject and are keen to find out more, but, if you are planning a lengthy undertaking such as a book you will probably have to do a considerable amount of research before approaching a publisher. None the less, the bulk of research will probably take place once you have gained a commission or at least a sign of interest from an editor and research is dealt with in more depth in chapter 6.

As well as convincing other parties that you know what you are talking about, some initial research will also give you a clearer idea of what angle or approach to take. As a general guideline, these are the things you should consider and aim to find out before you approach anyone:

- For profiles and person-based pieces, find out brief biographical details and where to find your interviewees (see next chapter for securing an interview), consider why they are interesting to write about for that publication, what aspect of them you intend to write about and as much information as possible about that aspect.
- For more general work where the interviewee is not the principal focus of the piece or which draws on a number of interviewees, you should have some idea of whom you are going to interview (such as members of the public or specialist opinion), how many people you are likely to consult, what angle you are intending to write about, how what you are going to write will benefit the publication and as much about your subject as possible.

Choosing a market

Once you have an idea of what you want to write and have chosen (as far as possible) who your interviewees are likely to be, the next step is to find an appropriate market. The choice of markets for journalists differs in many ways from the choice for those writing books and I have dealt with these separately under, respectively, *Choosing a magazine or paper* and *Choosing a publisher* in this chapter. If you are intending to conduct interviews for your personal interest or research and do not envisage publishing your work, this section will probably not be very relevant and you may want to skip forward to the next section on securing the interview itself.

Choosing a magazine or paper

Established freelance journalists often build up editorial contacts whom they can approach with a suitable idea, but, if you are a beginner or if you feel that your idea would not be suitable for a publication you have previously written for, you may need to look for a new market. For freelance journalists one of the best means of finding a good market is to have a lengthy browse through the magazine racks at a large newsagent. When choosing a publication for your piece look to see which magazines might be interested in your kind of article – there is no point in offering to do a profile piece to a magazine which never uses profiles. Some magazines favour homespun stories about the man or woman in your street, whilst others favour celebrity stories and some do a mixture of both. Some magazines have a regular slot for 'triumph over tragedy stories' or 'Day in the life of. . .' which may suggest possible features to you. If you are writing for a local publication such as your county magazine, the editor will probably be more interested in a profile on someone with a local connection rather than someone who is very famous but who has never visited the county. Whilst you can get a fairly good idea of the needs of a publication just by reading one issue, it is better to try to read several before approaching the market. The reading room in your library may contain backdated copies which you can read free of charge.

Target the reader

As well as considering the contents of the publication you will need to consider the needs of the readership. Ultimately, a magazine or paper is tailored to the needs of its readers (if it were not it would not survive). The litmus test for deciding on whether the article you intend to write is appropriate for the magazine is to ask and answer the questions: who is the reader and what do they want? You can build up a profile picture of the typical reader by looking at the contents of the magazine and considering what you think the age, gender, politics, socio-economic background, aspirations and so on of the average reader might be. Adverts can be particularly useful in helping you decide – a magazine that advertises porches is aimed at a particular kind of reader, whilst a magazine that advertises environmental pressure groups is aimed at another. When you have built up a picture in your own mind of the average reader you can ask what kind of interviewee would interest them. There is little point in offering a profile about an up-and-coming rock star to a retirement magazine (unless you have a particular slant which is of relevance to retired people – 'Why Sylvester Starshooter owes everything to his grandfather' may or may not be sufficient). Similarly an article on women's sexual fantasies would be more appropriate to magazines like *Cosmopolitan* or *Company* than *The Lady*.

Do they take freelance work?

If you are unsure as to whether the magazine or paper accepts freelance articles, look at the masthead where the in-house staff are listed. Often you will see a statement beneath the names of the staff to the effect that 'The editor welcomes submissions. . .' Sometimes the fact that the magazine considers manuscripts from freelancers is indicated by a disclaimer to the effect that 'The editor cannot accept responsibility for loss or damage to manuscripts whilst in his/her care'. For that read 'will consider my article'. Alternately it might say 'All unsolicited manuscripts must be accompanied by an SAE.' As well as looking at the publications at the newsagent you could also consult a reference work such as *Writers' & Artists' Yearbook* (A & C Black) or *The Writer's Handbook* (Macmillan). These books are updated annually and, as well as indicating which publications accept freelance articles, they offer guidelines as to the requirements of the most popular newspapers and magazines.

Multiple markets

If you are fairly new to article writing your goal may be just to have your intended article accepted and this is both a realistic and sensible plan. However, if you have already had some success in article writing and feel that you would really like to make freelancing pay, you may want to look at several markets for one interview (for more on multiple marketing see chapter 6, under *Research* and chapter 12). For most articles it is usually possible to find several potential markets but if your article is very specialised you may find that it will only be appropriate for one journal – 'A study of the effects of Mars retrograding over the Midheaven of People born under the sign of Capricorn during the Great Neptune, Uranus, Saturn conjunction' has limited potential for any market other than a fairly specialised astrological journal.

Angling

Before you approach a market you should have worked out a fairly clear idea as to the nature of the kind of piece you are going to write. Unless your idea is so novel that it has never been written about before or your subject is very hot property you will need to find an appropriate angle. It is pointless to approach an editor and say 'I'd like to write something about Mr X' because the editor is simply going to ask 'What about him?', if he bothers to ask anything at all. Editors need ideas and they need ideas that are relevant to the nature of their publication. Profile pieces are often welcome because they offer something new (as long as the person has not been interviewed for the publication previously) but you will still need to think of an appropriate angle that makes the piece relevant to the magazine – for instance, if you were interviewing a famous sportsman for a travel magazine you would need to focus more on his travels than his sporting achievements to make the profile appropriate to the publication. When choosing an angle try to think of something that is different, unusual and preferably a subject that the publication has not covered before. If you are intending to write for a particular publication you should read as many issues of it as possible to understand its nature and needs, but you cannot be expected to know about every feature that has ever been published. The answer is to ring up the editorial office (the telephone number will usually be listed at the front or back) and ask to be sent a features list. This will give you an edition by edition account of the features written in the current year and will give you a good idea of the kind of articles the publication wants.

Choosing a publisher

Whilst a full exposition of the ways to find a publisher is beyond the scope of this book, here are some basic guidelines. The most sensible approach to choosing a publisher is to look at their publications list. Ask your local library for a sight of the spring and autumn numbers of the *Bookseller* which consist of publishers' lists bound together. It would obviously be pointless to approach a publisher like Mills and Boon with an idea for a literary biography of George Eliot. Whatever your subject you will need to do a little preliminary research. If you are hoping to write a book on local history about the way people's lives were affected by the building of a large car factory in a largely rural area, you will need to look at other similar books (either in the local library or bookshop) to see which publishers may be interested in your idea. Tailor your approach to an appropriate publisher – if you would like to write someone's biography you will need to bear in mind that publishers of biographies of people like Jean-Paul Sartre might not be interested in a biography of your grandfather's boyhood in Edwardian England, fascinating though this may be. For information about which publishers are likely to consider new manuscripts consult *Writers' & Artists' Yearbook* or *The Writer's Handbook* which will also indicate the possible terms you can expect. A useful guide to writing non-fiction books is *The Way to Write Non-Fiction* by John Hines (Elm Tree Books).

Contacting the market

Most writers can manage to find and secure the co-operation of interview subjects and you may have already found a suitable person to interview before you contact the publication. If not, you will need to decide on your best way of proceeding. Writers planning to do a project which will involve a considerable amount of interviewing or who are totally reliant on getting a particular interview (a profile article for instance) are often faced with the chicken-and-egg situation of not knowing whom to approach first – the market or the interviewee – in the initial stages. On the one hand it may seem that there would be little point in approaching an editor or publisher with an idea if the main focus for your project (i.e. the interviewee) will not co-operate, while on the other hand you may feel reluctant to approach interviewees to say that you want to write about them if you have not already had a firm offer of publication. There are no hard and fast answers to this dilemma but it is always possible to go through a pilot stage before any commitments are made.

The pilot stage

The pilot stage is the point at which you begin to make tentative enquiries. In most instances it is better to approach the editor or publishers first with a suggestion – having the backing or at least the interest of an editor can help persuade your interviewees to give their co-operation. At this stage you may not be sure as to whether you can secure the appropriate interview and you should make this clear in your initial approach. Tell your prospective market that you hope to do an interview with your subject (include when and where if appropriate). Most publishers and editors are realists and will appreciate your situation if you are then unable to find the appropriate interviewee. In this case it is unlikely that you will be given a firm commission as there are no guarantees that you can deliver the goods, but you will at least find out if the editor is interested in your proposal. Not being able to produce the appropriate interviewee should not hinder you from writing for the same market again – after all, you have not entered into a contract or been commissioned. However, if you cannot get hold of a suitable interviewee it is important that you let the publication know.

If you are contacting your potential market by phone (see below) you should get a fairly quick response, but, if you have written and are waiting for a reply, you can save time by contacting your intended interviewee(s) in the meantime. Again your approach to the interviewee should be tentative as there has been no firm commission to write anything yet. Explain who you are and what you are hoping to do and ask whether they are willing to co-operate with you. At this point there are no commitments from anybody and you are simply clearing the way for your project to go ahead (for more on contacting interviewees see next chapter).

Making the approach – write or telephone?

Having an idea for a book accepted by a publisher tends to be a fairly lengthy process and it is usual to make a written approach in the first instance. For journalists who may have a sudden scoop or who may want to have a piece accepted for a particular deadline, it may make more sense to telephone, although writing is also usually perfectly acceptable and busy editors may prefer you to make initial contact by letter as this gives them time to think.

The letter

Writing a letter is in some ways easier than making a phone call – you avoid the possibility of being rejected on the spot, you are not under the same sort of pressure to get your words exactly right and you can take time over a letter until it meets with your approval.

If you choose to send a query letter to possible publishers asking if they would be interested in your proposal it is important that your letter helps to sell both you and your proposal. Letters should be written as business letters, typed and addressed to the editor in person if you know the name. It is now fairly standard to address an editor who is not known to you by both first and second name (e.g. 'Dear John Smith'). For the names of editors of magazines look under the masthead; for publishers try telephoning the office and asking for the name of the commissioning editor (numbers are available through directory enquiries or directories like *Writers' & Artists' Yearbook*). Editors and publishers are busy people and your letter should be both concise and informative. An initial query letter should cover the following:

- Explain what you propose to write about and the form it will take (a light humorous article, a profile, a thesis, etc.).
- Say why you think it would be an appropriate topic for the magazine/ publishing titles and/or why it might be a particular good idea to write something on this topic now (e.g. an article about war veterans to coincide with an anniversary).
- Say who your interviewees are (or are likely to be) and where and when you propose to see them (e.g. 'I intend to consult a number of experts in

the field/draw on the opinions of members of the public/interview a number of women who have had this experience/contact Sylvester Stardust when he stops off in London as part of his world tour/gather case histories from former workers at the car factory', etc. etc.).

- Explain briefly who you are, what your interest in the subject is and why you might be the right person to do it and anything you have written previously on the subject.

Certain letters will require more information but few should contain less (unless you are already known to the editor in which case you may want to forgo the fourth point). It is not necessary for a quick query letter to contain any more information than this and you can offer to provide more at a later date. However, for a lengthy undertaking like a book you may want to include an outline proposal, a personal CV and cuttings from previous writings and this will certainly not do any harm (although your CV should be reasonably potted – editors don't want to know about your egg and spoon race at primary school).

Telephoning (for journalists)

You may decide to telephone an editor because your proposed article requires urgent attention (possible reasons might be that your interviewee is about to go away on a world tour/you are interviewing men who take seasonal jobs by dressing up as Father Christmas and your article needs to be ready for the Christmas edition/you have just secured a world exclusive interview with Lord Lucan). Most editors will appreciate your pressing need and will listen to what you have to say – editors are in fact rarely rude but can be very hard to get hold of. If you are not put through to them, leave a message and a contact telephone number. If they are interested they will get back to you, so don't badger them unnecessarily – editors are busy people. Equally don't feel intimidated by the title 'editor'. Editors usually belong to the human species and many are heavily dependent on the work of freelancers for their publication. The editors of smaller magazines tend to be more approachable and may have more time at their disposal for you but do not take their time for granted. Keep your introduction short and to the point. It is often helpful to work out exactly what you are going to say beforehand and if you are nervous write it down in front of you.

> EXAMPLE I'm Joan Smith. I'm a freelance writer and I've just found out that a man down my street has won the National Lottery. He's particularly interesting because six years ago he was homeless and living on the streets. I know you sometimes do personal interest stories about people like him so I wondered if you would you be interested in seeing an article about him for *Bello*?
> You can fill in any more details later in the conversation.

If you are lucky, or equally if you have done your marketing well and your proposal is well suited to the needs of the publication, the editor may say 'yes' there and then. If you are an unknown, editors will probably not commit themselves to a commission but may say that they are interested and would like to see your piece. If this is the case you can ask them how soon they would like to see it – in this way you create an impression of professionalism and convey that you understand the meaning of the word 'deadline'. You can also check at this point whether the publication would need a photo for the piece by simply asking 'Do you need me to take a photo or do you use your own photographer?' Again this is a way of sounding professional and shows the editor that you have some understanding of the workings of the press industry. For more on photography see under chapter 8, *Conducting the interview*.

At this stage there is no commitment to publication but you have at least won some interest and you should follow this up. Don't waste time – do your interview and write it up whilst the editor is still likely to remember both you and your proposed piece.

If editors are unsure they may need more time to think and will either ask you to put your proposal in writing, ask you to ring at another time or say they will ring you or write to you. If they say 'no' outright it will usually be done politely and a reason given: 'Sorry we've already done that'. Don't be disheartened – it happens to everyone – just try another publication.

For advice on how to approach an interviewee when the editor has given you a 'maybe' or if you have not secured a market first, see next chapter.

On spec

Whilst most established writers write for commissions to save time, energy and rejection slips, new writers often have to begin by sending off speculative pieces. It is difficult to gain a commission if you have no track record in writing and can also be difficult to gain a track record if you have not got a commission. The only answer to this Catch 22 situation is to remind yourself that everyone has to start somewhere and that, if your work and your ideas are good enough, you will get the break you need. Even if you have had no writing experience or published work to your name so far, it is often worth just trying to get a sign of interest or a 'maybe' from an editor. Alternatively you can simply send off your piece with an enquiry letter and see what happens. Replies from editors can often take several weeks and the fact that they do not reply straight away does not mean that they are not interested. If you have done some careful market research, written to a good standard and tailored your interview to the needs of the publication, you should stand a reasonable chance.

5
GETTING THE INTERVIEW

Unless you are interviewing a close friend or relative (for more on this see below under *Family and friends*) or know exactly whom you are going to interview and how to find them, you will need to track down the right person to interview. In this chapter I have outlined a number of possible ways of finding the right person but how you eventually get to meet your subject may be quite surprising as the following story illustrates. A colleague who was writing a thesis on women who worked on a particular railway line during the Second World War found that going through all the conventional sources had yielded nothing. Feeling rather disillusioned she went out into the garden where her gardener was pruning the hedges. He observed that she looked fed up and she explained what the problem was. It transpired that the man's wife had worked on the railway in the War. Seemingly quite by chance my colleague had found the contact she needed. Perhaps the moral of the story is: don't limit yourself to searching for interviewees through conventional channels – sometimes just mentioning what you need in conversation can yield you the right person.

Family and friends
A good way to begin learning and practising interview skills is to start on those nearest to you. Close friends and relatives can provide an excellent source of interview material which is readily available and easy to find. Journalists in particular may often interview people they know simply for convenience and this is fine for articles which need to draw on a cross-section of general opinion or if you already know people who would be suitable interviewees for the kind of article you want to write – it is just as easy to interview your husband and men friends for an article about the ten things men look for most in a marriage as it is to go out and interview complete strangers. In this way you can sometimes conduct interviews without having to step beyond your front door. But whilst there is much to be said in favour of starting off interviewing with a few friendly and familiar guinea pigs, if you want to interview on a regular basis you will eventually need to turn your attention to the world inhabitants beyond your threshold. Not only will your friends and relatives become a little jaded if they are the sole subjects for your interviews, but you will also find that they just might not be the most appropriate people to interview or will limit you to only interviewing about certain subjects.

Finding an interviewee

This section deals with how to track down subjects to interview when you do not have a ready-made contact address or phone number. Below are just some methods which can help you track down your subject, but bear in mind that there are as many ways to find an interviewee as there are interviewees. For people in the public eye or in a relatively high position you will usually need to go through an intermediary such as an agent, press officer or secretary, whilst you would normally approach ordinary people in person. As a general guideline, the more feelers you put out when trying to find the right person, the more likely you are to find them and, if you are prepared to ask and phone around as many sources as possible, you will almost certainly find someone who is suitable for your purpose. If your interviewee is unknown to you or you do not actually know exactly whom you need to approach, it is often a good idea to trawl as widely as possible, starting with a broad search and narrowing down. In practice you may find that you only need to go through one or two sources to locate the ideal person but experiences can vary from one search to another. Do not assume that you always have to contact the largest or most prestigious institutions. A telephone call to one in your nearest town may suffice – a brain surgeon from Bogmoor on Sea is just as likely to be able to answer an enquiry about brain surgery as is one from a top London hospital. Unless you want very specialised advice, start with the handiest source.

Useful directories

If you do not have a particular interviewee in mind but know you would like to interview someone about a particular subject, a good starting point will be the reference works in your library. Most libraries have a number of directories which provide invaluable information, including telephone numbers and contact names, of potentially useful people. Amongst the more helpful ones are *Dod's Parliamentary Companion* which gives details of and contact numbers and addresses for members of the House of Lords and the House of Commons and includes special interests of members; *Councils, Committees and Boards* is a 'handbook of advisory, consultative, executive and similar bodies in British public life'; *Centres and Bureaux* is a 'directory of effort, information and expertise'; *Charities Digest* offers details and contact numbers for charities; *Major Companies Guide*; *The Voluntary Agencies Directory* provides contacts within the voluntary sector and *Trade Associations and Professional Bodies of the United Kingdom* is another valuable resource. *Current British Directories* is a guide to all directories published in the British Isles and could be a good starting point if you are stuck, as is *Whitaker's Almanac*. See *Booklist* for further details of these publications. There are many more potentially useful directories and, if you need help, ask a librarian. Librarians are trained to help you find the information you need or at least to point you in the right direction. A friendly neighbourhood librarian is invaluable for any kind of research. See next chapter for more on libraries.

Press officers

Many large institutions and companies (ranging from the royal family to the local council) employ a press officer whose job is to promote and represent the company and to deal with enquiries from members of the media and other writers. Most companies and organisations prefer you, as a writer, to go through the proper channels by contacting the press office first, as the press officer is specifically trained to deal with the kind of enquiries you are likely to make or will at least be able to suggest someone else who is best able to help you. A friendly press officer can be an invaluable source of information. If you want to interview a managing director of a computer company, but do not know the name of any in person, you could ask the press officer of the appropriate trade or professional organisation to suggest someone. Smaller companies and organisations may not employ a press officer but this role is often fulfilled by the personnel department, so try that. Press office numbers are usually readily available – if you have a company in mind, ring them directly and ask to be put through to the press office. Alternatively try Directory Enquiries. When ringing press officers tell them your name, the name of your publication and/or your purpose for ringing and have a pen and paper ready to take down information. If you want to interview someone about events abroad a good starting point will be the information officer at the appropriate embassy or high commission – numbers are available in the library or through Directory Enquiries. When speaking to a press officer it is important to remember that they are there to promote the company they work for and may present a more rosy picture than is actually the case. Bear this in mind when you speak to them – if you have researched your subject thoroughly (see next chapter) you will be in a position to challenge them.

Entertainers and agents

Many entertainers of many varieties use an agent and these should be your first port of call when trying to track down stars of the screen and stage. Spotlight is an organisation which can provide free contact numbers of theatrical agents and has listings of literally thousands of actors, actresses and production personnel. The telephone number is 0171-437 7631. The role of agents is to look after and help promote their clients and their work so if you are helping them to fulfil this role in any way (and most kinds of writing count as promotion), your enquiry will probably meet with a positive outcome. However, particularly in the case of highly successful stars, the agent may also be helping to protect them from too much public scrutiny or distractions from their work, so don't assume that they will always be able to fix up an interview for you. It is unfortunate that sometimes the nature of your publication will influence whether you get an interview or not – a writer for a glossy magazine will probably stand more chance of getting an interview with a major Hollywood actor than would a writer for the *Crumford Chronicle* (in this case the person writing for the *Crumford Chronicle* would probably not have adequately researched the market anyway).

Tracking down a star might be a lengthy process with no result and it is probably better to start your interviewing career with a few rising hopefuls before moving on to the big names. An alternative to contacting agents is to get on the press list of your nearest city theatre (many city theatres attract biggish names), as these sometimes offer press conferences to promote the show, so you may be able to interview a star that way (see also *Press conferences* in chapter 2). If you are stuck, remember to trawl widely – ringing round the box offices of theatres might seem a leap in the dark but you may find someone who knows someone who can give you the agent's name of a leading lady. One directory which lists agents is *Artistes and Agents* (Richmond House).

Writers

If you want to contact writers you should get in touch with the publishers of their book(s) and ask if they have an agent. You can then telephone or write to the agent who will either put you directly in touch with the writer or will forward your information to them. Sometimes the publishers themselves act as semi-agents and can give you the author's address or phone number (this is because the author and publishers have usually come to an agreement that the author's name can be given out to specific enquirers). If you are promoting an author's book(s) you will usually find that your enquiry gets a good response. As with phoning a press officer, give your name, publication and/or reason for calling. For addresses of publishers look inside the cover of the author's book or look in *Writers' & Artists' Yearbook* or *The Writer's Handbook*.

VIPs

If you need to contact royalty go through the Royal Press Office. Your chances of getting a personal interview are minimal to the point of non-existent but the spokesperson may be able to supply you with the information you need. Some titled people, particularly the landed and estated kind, employ an agent or manager and some are listed in directories which you will find in the library. You could try ringing the ancestral home and asking to speak to the estate manager in the first instance, although sometimes you may get put through directly. For the number of the house contact Directory Enquiries or look through one of the many guidebooks to the nation's national treasures.

The personal approach

There are occasions when it is perfectly reasonable to approach well-known people in person and ask if they'd be prepared to give you an interview either then or in the future. Places where this could happen are usually publicity events which could include authors attending signing sessions in a book shop (they will probably be more willing if you buy their book first), promotional events (National Poetry Day), public readings or exhibitions, conferences, etc. Approaching someone in person takes a lot of courage but can often yield good results for those who dare. Wait for a suitable moment – preferably when there is a lull in activity – before approaching but don't allow the moment to pass. Say who you are and why you would like to interview them (in cases like this you may not already have a market lined up but you could introduce yourself as a freelance writer and say which publication you would like to interview them for). If they agree to be interviewed set up a time and a place and let them go about their business once you have secured the interview.

NOTE This does not mean that if you see a celebrity rock star shopping in Tesco you are entitled to go up and interview him there and then – the famous deserve their privacy when not working as much as the rest of us and, if you want to interview them you should go through the proper channels.

Contacting experts

If you need an expert opinion but don't know any relevant experts, you could try contacting one through their place of work. If, for example, you need to speak to a gynaecologist, ring your nearest hospital, get the name from the receptionist and ask to be put through to the consultant's secretary. For academic experts try the relevant department of a university (most libraries contain university and college prospectuses where you can find both departments and telephone numbers). Go through the departmental secretary initially. Many experts have written books so you may be able to contact them through their publisher or agent (see above) and having an opinion from a famous expert is more of a scoop than from a backroom one. Don't worry if the first person you try is not available – experts tend to be busy people – just try someone else. Many experts love to have their sense of their own expertise confirmed by an enquiry from someone who may be promoting their expertise even further. If you do not know where to start looking, try ringing a relevant association (there are associations for every-thing from embalmers to embryologists) and ask to be put in touch with someone appropriate. You can get the numbers of professional societies from the library or, if you know the exact title of the society, from Directory Enquiries. If you do not feel happy about telephoning them directly, you could write a letter (see below) and in some cases this may be more appropriate, particularly if you are not in a pressing hurry to get the information, need a lot of information or are contacting them for complex reasons. Additionally, a letter is in many ways less invasive. If, for example, you are writing a thesis and want to draw on the expertise of a specialist in your field, it is usually more acceptable to write in the first instance.

Advertising for interviewees

If you do not have anything to lead you to your choice of interview subjects, you could always try advertising. Where you advertise will depend on your choice of subject. Someone who wants to interview anyone who knew W. H. Auden in his later years might start by placing an advert in a publication such as *The Times Literary Supplement* (they would, of course, be trying other sources at the same time such as publishers and academics). If, for instance, you wanted to interview people who had been present at the excavation of a prehistoric site near a particular town forty years previously, you would probably want to place your advert in the town's local paper. Sometimes you may need to be both a little creative and to refine down your research – people who were present at an excavation forty years previously might have reached retirement age. Are there any clubs for pensioners in the area where you could advertise? Does the location of the site lead you to think that people from a particular area of the town or a neighbouring village were more likely to be there? Is there a school near the site whose local school children may have gone to watch – does the school have any past records of the event? Are there any newspaper cuttings of the event in a local paper which could suggest possibilities? The local archaeological society and the county council archaeology department should also be able to offer some useful leads.

If you want to contact someone who lives locally, don't forget the library which will probably have a notice board where you can advertise. The best way to achieve results from advertising is to look at as many possibilities as you can and advertise in as many places as possible (time and money permitting). Your advert need only be short and simple:

> Local author researching the excavation of the White Donkey figure on Benson Hill would be interested to hear from anyone who witnessed the event or knows of anyone who witnessed it for a local history book. All information gratefully received. Please contact. . .

You can leave either your own telephone number and address or use a post box.

Published letter

The letters page of a publication may be willing to print a letter asking for subjects who are prepared to be interviewed. Tracking people down through the letters page is fairly common in regional papers and is often used when someone wants to contact old school colleagues for a reunion and for similar events, but there is no reason why you should not try to find interviewees in this way. You could also try writing to specialist interest magazines. If, for instance, you wanted to write a piece on the education of children who grew up on coal barges on the canals earlier this century you could try writing to a magazine like *Canal and Riverboat* or *Waterways World*, asking if anyone has any knowledge or experience of the subject and leaving a forwarding address. The advantage of writing a letter is that it is free and can reach a wide and appropriate audience. The disadvantage is that demands on page space will determine whether or not your letter gets published. Whilst there is no guarantee that the letter will yield your subject(s) to you, it may well spark off a memory in someone who was not directly involved but knows someone who was, or even knows someone who knows someone. This means that your research is under way and you are gradually homing in on your subject(s).

Approaching magazines

Contacting a specialist magazine could prove a useful source of information, both for getting in touch with an expert (the editor him/herself might be an appropriate interviewee) or for making contact with a contributor whom it may be useful to interview. The publication may not be prepared to hand out names and personal addresses, feeling a duty to protect individual privacy, but will probably be prepared to forward a letter for you or suggest a good place to contact someone – for instance, a sports magazine might be able to put you in touch with an athlete's trainer or at least give the name of the training ground. You could try ringing in the first instance (get the number by looking inside a copy of a magazine) or send a letter to be forwarded. Always include a covering letter explaining the purpose, why you need to contact this person and expressing thanks for the anticipated help. Don't forget to put a stamp on the forwarding letter. Enclose an SAE for the intended recipient.

Knocking on doors

Sometimes the simplest thing to do is just to go to a likely place and ask if there is anyone who can help you. For ordinary people who live near, you could try knocking on the door or telephoning. Don't assume that they will have time to spare there and then, but explain what you are doing and see if they will agree to meet you at a later date. This will give them time to think it over and not feel pressurised. If you want to interview elderly people for a local history project, you could try approaching an old people's home or a pensioner's club. The staff may be able to put you in touch with people who are potentially useful.

Institutions

You may be able to find the person you need to interview by contacting a relevant institution – football grounds, sports clubs, theatres, museums and so on all might be able to help you get in touch with the right person. If in doubt trawl widely and narrow down to the person you need.

Vox-pop

When you are doing a vox-pop-type interview on a particular subject you need to choose an area where you are likely to meet the right people to talk about the subject. For instance, if you want to write an article about an accident black spot in your town, go to the place where it is and approach people with a view to finding anyone who regularly uses the area and who may have something to say about it. Aim for a variety of people – pedestrians, cyclists and motorists (assuming you can find the latter stationary). For more general vox-pops, a busy shopping precinct is often a fruitful source, especially if you can find people sitting on benches who may have time on their hands to talk to you.

Ask your interviewee

If you are doing several interviews or are conducting research on a large scale, a very important way of getting in touch with interviewees is to ask the people you are already interviewing if they can suggest anyone else who might be able to help you. Out of politeness it is as well to say that you want to interview other people on something slightly different from the contents of the present interview, but don't feel bound by this in practice. If your interviewees are experts they will doubtless have access to a number of potentially useful people and you should get their names, addresses and phone numbers before you leave.

Last but not least

Don't overlook the obvious. One of my first interviews as a freelance journalist was with a well-known writer whose works had been serialised on television and who had developed into something of a local celebrity. I did not then know that the proper approach would have been to go through the agent (in fact it turned out that he didn't have one) and was unsure as to how to go about tracking him down, although I knew roughly which area he lived in. Even though I was very new to interviewing, knocking on doors did not seem a particularly appropriate way to approach him, given that I was interested in writing a feature article, not an urgent news item. I therefore decided to start with the obvious and work outwards. The obvious choice was the telephone directory, although I was certain that he would be ex-directory. I decided to look on the very off chance and there he was. I rang up, he answered the phone and an interview was arranged. Simple as that. Whilst now I would almost certainly go through more official channels for someone like that, simply looking people up in the telephone directory can be a fruitful source of interviews. (*See* below for telephoning.)

Your contact book

When tracking down interviewees keep a record of all useful names, addresses, phone numbers, directories, press offices, associations and organisations encountered en route for future reference in your contact book. You never know when you might need them again and by recording the information you can save yourself a lot of research time in the future.

Approaching – write or telephone

When you have found out how to contact your interviewee, you need to make arrangements for the interview. The procedure is similar to arranging a market for your work. Whether you write to or telephone a potential interviewee is a matter for your discretion. Journalists who need to meet a tight copy deadline might prefer to phone. If you are planning to write a biography of someone and feel that a particular source might be very helpful, but think you will need to spend a lot of time on the interview, it might be better to write in the first instance outlining what you require.

Telephone

Preparation

Before telephoning you need to make sure that you are adequately prepared both practically and psychologically. For practical purposes make sure that you have a piece of paper and a pen that works ready to hand so that you can record any necessary details such as addresses and times of meetings. At this stage of the proceedings you may not have all the information you need but you should be sufficiently well briefed to talk competently about why you want to do the interview. Make sure that you are clear about what you want to say or ask – confusion or hesitation creates a bad impression. It may help to write down what you want to say before you start.

You will nearly always get a better response if you can inject a friendly and confident tone into your voice. When people are anxious (as is usually the case when arranging the first few interviews), this is quite difficult to achieve so you may find it helpful to practise beforehand. See how many different ways you can say 'I'd like to interview you' – try being curt, polite, unfriendly, friendly, angry, sad, etc. Try to register how the way you speak affects what you say (it's sometimes helpful to practise on a friend) – decide which approach you like best and which you like least. Your potential interviewees will be making similar assessments, although they may not be consciously aware of it. Smiling down the phone as you speak will often have a beneficial effect on your tone.

The opening line

If you decide to telephone people because of their profession, ring them at work – phoning people in the privacy of their own home about the work they thought they'd left behind at the office does not always go down very well. If you are ringing people for other reasons – perhaps they have witnessed an accident – you will probably have to ring them at home. Keep your opening line brief and to the point:

> Hallo, I'm Ann Author, I'm currently writing a book on macramé for Folded Paper Publications. I spoke to the editor of *Macramé World* and she suggested that you might be a useful person to talk to because you've had over twenty years experience of exhibiting your macramé. I was wondering whether it would be possible to arrange to talk to you about it?

In this example you have stated who you are, what you are writing for, how you got in touch with the person (via the editor of *Macramé World*) and have stated your reason for ringing. It is quite important to remember when telephoning that the time might not be exactly convenient for the person on the other end. This is particularly the case if you are intending to conduct a telephone interview (see chapter 6) which may take up some time, so you should always check whether this is a convenient time and, if not, ask when is.

If you are not entirely sure whom you need to speak to, the patter is the same as the above (or similar), but add something like 'I'm interested in talking to anyone who can help me with a book I'm researching on macramé. Can you suggest anyone who may be able to help me?'

If the editor said maybe

If you are unknown to editors it is unlikely that they will have given you a definite commission for an article but they may have said that they will look at your piece. In this case it would be unwise to say to your prospective interviewee 'I'm writing this for the *Thames Times*' unless you are very sure that it will be accepted. In this case it is usually better to say something like 'The editor of the Thames Times is very interested in doing a piece about. . .'

No specific market

If you have not secured an editor's interest beforehand you could say something like 'I write for a number of freelance markets and I think the editor of *Thames Times* would be very interested in a piece about. . .' or 'I'm hoping to sell this to *Thames Times* as they have shown a lot of interest in this kind of thing. . .'

The follow-up

If people are used to being approached for interviews, they will probably take your call in their stride, but some may become quite flustered so take your time to explain to them exactly what it is you want and why. Give them time to ask questions. If you need a photo from your interviewee, you may want to mention it at this point as you explain more about the interview. Do not try to use the name of your publication to impress people or to make yourself sound important – it is surprising how many people think that the printed word is something very special and people who write very clever – your job is to encourage the interviewees to say 'yes', not to make them feel like lesser human beings. Most people find being asked to give an interview quite flattering and will probably be eager to help. Nine times out of ten your subjects will say 'yes' (some may say 'yes' as if you had just offered them a million dollars). Often your biggest selling point will be that you can offer them some benefit such as publicity. This may be personal promotion or the promotion of a product or company. If it is appropriate, mention the possible benefits to them: for example, 'The magazine reaches a monthly readership of 40 000 people who will have a specific interest in what you have to say' – you can check readership figures from '*The Writer's Handbook*'. Anyone with a commercial turn of mind will probably have already worked out the potential benefits.

A time and place

If they have said 'yes' and you are intending to conduct a face-to-face interview, you should fix up a time, date and place to meet them. Interviews can take place almost anywhere but in practice you will usually see someone either at home or at the place of work. If you are interviewing subjects because their job confers a certain expertise – a captain of industry or a trapeze artist – you would probably go to see them at their place of work. Apart from the fact that you are seeing them in the context for which you are interested in them, this would also give them the chance to demonstrate to you their relevant workplace skills where necessary. If you are interviewing someone for more personal details – for example, talking to an old soldier about his wartime experience, you would probably find it best to talk to him in his own home where he is most comfortable. For interviewing in pubs and restaurants see chapter 9, *In the event of. . .*

Remember that it is you the interviewer who should accommodate the interviewees – if they can only see you late in the evening, then you should go along with that. Ask them when and where is convenient. If they are not sure, make a suggestion such as 'I could meet you at work/at your home. . .'

Many interviewees will want to know when you need to do the interview by or when your deadline is – say when you would prefer to have it done by and most people will be happy to accommodate you as far as they can. Sometimes a person may be very busy and may not be able to see you for a while. If this is going to make it impossible for you to meet your deadline, say so and hope that an earlier day might be arranged. If this is not possible you will need to renegotiate a deadline with your editor or choose a different interviewee. Let your interviewee know approximately how long the interview is likely to last. If you don't know, give an estimate – overestimate rather than underestimate but do not expect to be given more than an hour from someone who is really busy, unless you are arranging an interview a long time in advance. Whilst some people may be willing to give you all day, don't assume that everyone can drop everything to talk to you. Check with your interviewee whether they can give the required amount of time. If not, reschedule the interview. For a full-length profile article you will probably need to set aside a minimum of at least one hour and probably longer. In practice, once an interview is under way and you have established a good rapport your interviewee will probably be happy to talk to you for longer than you had originally planned but don't count on this for everybody. For arranging a second interview see under chapter 9, *In the event of. . .*

As soon as you have arranged the time, date and place write them down and, before you ring off, check once more with your interviewee to make sure that both of you have got the same details. If you are not familiar with the area where you are supposed to meet, ask for directions and, if you are intending to drive to the interview, check that you will be able to park nearby. A twenty-minute walk from a parking place could mean arriving late. When everything is arranged, say 'thank you' and ring off.

If they hesitate

Probably the majority of people you approach will agree to be interviewed but there are occasions when someone may be uncertain about whether to give you an interview or not. There may be many reasons for this, shyness, insecurity or previous bad interview experiences being just a few. Most people find making a direct refusal quite difficult over the phone and this can give you a certain amount of room for manoeuvre. If, for instance, people hesitate out of a feeling of unworthiness (and this is not unusual when dealing with ordinary people who are not used to being the subject of interviews), you may need to persuade them that they have a valuable contribution to make to your piece. Below are some examples of ways in which you can do this, although obviously every case is different and you may need to do a certain amount of thinking on your feet in some cases:

- For those who feel they haven't got anything useful to say: 'I'd be really interested to hear what you have to say because you were there at the time/fit exactly into the category of people I want to talk to/obviously you know a lot more about it than I do. . .'

- For those people who feel that there might be other people who would be better: 'I'm interested in talking to as wide a variety of people as possible because no two people's experiences are the same, so your contribution would be just as valuable as everyone else's. . .'
- For people who are afraid that the interview might be a horrendous ordeal/they are going to be held up to public scrutiny/the interviewer is going to try to worm out all their worst secrets. . . : 'I'd just like to have a little chat with you really. It's all very informal and you don't have to tell me anything you don't want to. . .'
- For people who think every journalist writes for the tabloids and for people who want to know more about what they'll be doing before they agree: 'If you like, I can send you a copy of the magazine/paper so you can see the kind of thing we're interested in before we meet'. In this case you are still working on the assumption that the interview is going to go ahead which will have a persuasive action on the person you are talking to. Try to sound as relaxed and confident and professional as possible – the effects will rub off on them.

They say 'no'

It is rare for people to say 'no' outright without an explanation. When this happens it is usually because they have had a very bad interview experience previously (a tabloid journalist snooping through their underwear whilst allegedly using the bathroom), are experiencing other problems at the time or have a serious personality defect. It may be all three. Either way try not to take it personally. If this happens at your first interview attempt, you have simply been very unfortunate, but don't let it deprive you of all the wonderful interviews you may have in the future. If someone is adamant that the answer is 'no', there is not much you can do about it – after all no one is under any obligation to grant you an interview and it is you who is asking for the favour. If someone says 'no' and gives a reason, you may still have room for manoeuvre:

EXAMPLE

INTERVIEWEE: Sorry but I'm going off to the Bahamas this afternoon.

YOU: Do you have time for a five-minute chat over the phone?

or

That's no problem. Do you think we could do it when you get back?

EXAMPLE

INTERVIEWEE: I'm sorry but I'm not the right person to ask really – that's not my department

YOU: That's fine, I'm sorry to have bothered you but could you suggest anyone else in your field who may be able to help?

EXAMPLE

INTERVIEWEE: I don't usually give interviews...

YOU (tricky one this): Yes, I've met a few people who've said that – some of them have just had bad interview experiences or some people feel it would be too invasive. Would you consider doing an interview if we stuck to certain terms?

In the last example you have opened up the way for a possible dialogue and once you get people talking you are more likely to persuade them to give you an interview. You have also reinforced the fact that they can have some say in the proceedings. This may preclude you from asking certain things but at least you may get your interview.

Some people may want time to think it over and may ask you to ring again later. This is perfectly within reason. It is important at this stage that you work out a mutually convenient time to ring. In this way you 'hook' your interviewee without being overtly forceful. Just say something like: 'That's fine – when is it a good time for me to ring you?'

Sometimes they may ask if they can ring you back. This puts you slightly at their mercy as they may not actually ring you. It is a good idea to try to tie them down to a specific time or try to manoeuvre things so that you are the one who is doing the ringing: 'I'm not going to be very easy to get hold of on my usual number in the next few days – would it be possible for me to ring you when you've had time to think about it?'

The three Ps
Throughout the telephone conversation – even if you are refused an interview – remember the three Ps. You should be:
- Polite
- Persistent
- Professional

Letters
Writing to your chosen subject is a more sedate way of securing an interview and is used by many writers. By writing you allow your prospective inter-viewee more time to digest the contents and the full implications of what you are asking of them. Writing may also feel less invasive to some people. The big disadvantages of writing are that you will probably have to wait longer for a reply (you may in some cases get no reply at all) and it is often easier to say 'no' by letter than over the phone where you can use your persuasive skills if you think someone is wavering.

As with telephoning you will need to be polite and professional in your approach to create the best impression. Your letter should be typed in business-letter style (if you're not sure about this consult one of the many books available on business English which you should be able to find in the library). Remember to include the date, telephone number and postcode. Using headed paper creates a professional impression but don't become over concerned about this. Your letter should be concise and to the point, whilst giving the reader a sufficient idea of what you want. Say who you are, why you are writing, what your publication is (where relevant) and how you come to be in contact with the recipient. Suggest that you meet at a time and place which is convenient for the subject, or, if you are likely to be in the area, suggest that you meet then. Finish by expressing your thanks for the anticipated help. It is good manners to enclose an SAE if you are expecting a written reply and sometimes it is reasonable to suggest making a reverse telephone call to you – particularly if this is an overseas communication.

No reply

If your letter fails to elicit a response after a reasonable interval (this is a matter for personal judgement), you have two choices – you can either give up on the interview (although this would be a pity if the failure to reply was caused by nothing more than a letter going astray in the post) or you can try writing or phoning again. If you decide to write or phone, do not do so in an aggressive or reproachful way. No one owes you an interview and no one is obliged to reply to your letter, no matter how polite and accommodating you were. Simply remind your potential interviewee that you have been in touch previously and repeat your request for an interview. Most people will probably feel rather guilty at this stage and may be particularly willing to help you. Be understanding if they say they have been under enormous work pressure (perhaps they have) and say that it doesn't matter that they haven't got back to you (even if it does), but could you arrange something now please. If they still fail to respond, you may have to reconsider them as a choice of interviewee or give up.

Getting past secretaries and receptionists

A doctor friend once told me that medical receptionists are trained to keep the patients away from the doctors. Whilst this may have been said tongue slightly in cheek, most of us have come up against obstructive secretaries and receptionists at one point and this may happen when you are trying to arrange an interview. Don't get cross with them (they're probably only doing their job), but do be persistent, stress the importance of what you're doing and be prepared to keep ringing back until you are put through. A process of erosion usually works.

Practical considerations

In an ideal world we would all be able to contact an interviewee any time we wanted and carry out the interview immediately. However, in the real world there are sometimes obstacles which may make interviewing a particular choice of subject unfeasible and you may have to reluctantly give up on the idea. If you are a freelance journalist you cannot always guarantee that the paper or magazine you write for will pay for such things as travel expenses and overnight stays. It may not therefore be worth your while to travel several hundred miles to interview someone when the travel expenses alone could eat into and beyond the profit you are expecting to make from the article itself. If the editor is not prepared to pay up you may have to abandon the idea, no matter how good a 'scoop' you feel it might have been.

Sometimes your subjects may not be readily available as they are travelling around the world or are indisposed through illness. If you can afford to wait and think it would be worthwhile to do so by all means wait, but sometimes it is just more practical to use an alternative subject or change plans altogether. If, however, you feel that your piece cannot possibly be written without the co-operation of a particular person, and you are already far committed to it, waiting for them to become available may be your only course of action (or inaction). Except in cases of unforeseen mortality, most subjects can be tracked down eventually.

An alternative to seeing someone in person is to write or telephone – if you were living in London and needed to get hold of an expert in New York, but felt that a trip to America was beyond your budget and/or time limits, you could try conducting an interview by phone or letter. For more on interviewing by letter see chapter 2, *Types of interview*, and for telephone interviews see chapter 8, *Conducting the interview*.

6
PREPARATION BEFORE THE INTERVIEW

The next two chapters look at the ways in which you can best prepare yourself, practically and mentally, for the interview. No interview will ever turn out exactly as you expect it to and a few interviews may throw up the completely unexpected, but by making the initial preparations set out below you should be able to cope with most interviews, avoid avoidable mistakes and get as much out of your interview as possible.

Whilst it might be a slight exaggeration to say that good interviewing is 99 per cent preparation and 1 per cent inspiration, the ratio of good preparation to a successful interview is very high.

When you have arranged a market for your work (where appropriate) and fixed up a time, date and place for your interview, you have already done a lot of the groundwork, but there is still some work to do before you are ready for the actual interview.

Research
Unless you are already very well-versed in your subject, you will need to do some research before doing the interview. Journalists in particular may find that they need to become an overnight expert on something they know nothing about, whilst other writers will need to home in on and bone up on information that may be specifically relevant to the forthcoming interview.

Why research?
There are several reasons why some preliminary research is usually necessary and below are a few of them:
- Interviews take place within a finite amount of time and it is better to use this time to talk about important matters that are central to your writing rather than to waste time finding out basic information which is readily available outside the interview. There is no point in asking a question like 'What school did you go to?' when a bit of basic research can provide a question like: 'In what way did going to one of Britain's leading public schools influence your career choice?' Good research generates informed, intelligent and relevant questions.
- As an interviewer you are under an obligation to take an interest in your subject (even if this is asking the managing director of a sewage firm about prospects for the industry). Part of showing an interest is having some knowledge about what or who is being discussed. It is both bad interview practice and bad manners to ask obviously uninformed questions of the 'What was your home town, Mrs Thatcher?' type.

It can also prove embarrassing: 'Would you say that last year was a good one for the company?' 'No three of our factories had to close down and over a thousand people were made redundant.'

- The more informed you are, the more professional you appear and the more you are likely to get a good response from your interviewee.
- If you have done some research you are in a much better position to deal with issues which may arise in the course of an interview. You are less likely to become confused or thrown off course if you have made the effort to learn about and understand your subject. Moreover an interview becomes much more interesting when you have prepared for it.
- You are in a much better position to spot something new, revealing or challenging if you have studied your subject beforehand.

EXAMPLE

INTERVIEWEE: We've decided to let women become full members of the club as of next year.

YOU: But I understood that you were strongly opposed to the idea – I read in a paper that you said that it would never happen in your life-time.

INTERVIEWEE: Well I'm not over the moon about it but it's what most members want and I suppose we have to move with the times as much as everyone else. . .

- In the course of researching your subject you may find other possible openings to write about. For freelance journalists, financial survival is often dependent on getting as much mileage as possible from an idea for an article. Effective freelancing means being able to sell your idea to a wide range of markets and to do this you will need to get several different angles. Often an angle will be thrown up in the process of your research – for instance you may find that the famous painter you are going to interview: is of retirement age (possibilities for a retirement magazine); has twenty cats (animal magazines); lives on a canal boat for three months of the year (waterways or boating magazine); used to be a cobbler (shoe-making trade magazine possibly).

The wider you research the more fruitful your interview is likely to be.

Where to research

An extensive overview of research facilities is not possible within the confines of this book but for an excellent introduction to research sources see *Research for Writers* by Ann Hoffmann (A & C Black). What follows is a brief outline of some starting points for research.

The library

The best place for any writer or researcher to start is likely to be the reference section of the library. Every serious writer or researcher should familiarise themselves with the contents. Whilst your library may not yield exactly the information you want, it can very often point you in the direction you need to take for your research. If you are unsure, ask the librarian to show you how to use the library's research facilities and latest information technology.

Use your library as much as possible – it's a writer's best friend. If the information you require is particularly obscure or specialised, you may want to consult a specialist library or a major reference library. For more on this see *Book list*.

Cuttings libraries

Many local newspaper offices have cuttings libraries where subjects covered in the publication are filed and stored. If, for example, you needed to trace the history of the closure of a factory before interviewing an unemployed worker, this might be a good place to start. Some newspaper offices will let you use their library for a small fee. To make enquiries telephone the appropriate newspaper office. The main national collection for newspapers is the British Library Newspaper Library (Colindale Avenue, London NW9 5HE; tel: 0171 323 7353). If your local library has a reading room you will probably be able to get hold of back-dated copies of some newspapers and magazines and many libraries will provide index journals of previous publications.

Researching people

If people are well known, they will doubtless have been written about in one form or another. The most fruitful source for your research will be a biography or autobiography which will also yield other potential contacts whom you may want to interview. Useful sources for finding out the essential details of the rich, famous and talented can be found in the reference section of the library. The classic is *Who's Who*. There are many specialised forms of biographical reference works, including those for professions, artists, sports people, etc., and your librarian should be able to suggest some to you. If someone has written a book, you will probably find a helpful resume of them on the blurb of a jacket cover which will be a good starting point.

You should research the work of artists, actors, writers *et al.* as well as their life histories. Do this as thoroughly as possible – look for reviews of the work, go and see their exhibitions, see the movies, read the books, anything except wear the tee shirt to the interview. Sometimes agents and publishers can provide useful information about their client (known as a press pack which includes biographical information) but you should bear in mind that this is likely to be promotional, so take it with a pinch of salt. Trawl through cuttings libraries, consult newspaper and magazine indexes. If you can find any previous articles about your interviewee draw on the information they contain, but don't waste time asking the same questions that produced that information.

Information on a subject

Challenge – name a subject that has never been written about. There are books on everything under the ozone layer and the quickest way to find them is through your local library. A quick easy reference source might be the *Encyclopedia Britannica* or any encylopaedia or dictionary derivative. You can get bare bone details of companies, organisations and charities from the reference works listed under *Useful directories* in the previous chapter. Most press offices can provide up-to-the-minute information about the organisation or people they represent and they will usually be willing to send you this through the post. Alternatively you could speak to the press officer in person, thus doing a mini interview before you do the big one.

No information available

It may happen from time to time, in particular if you are interviewing ordinary people, that there is no information available about them at all. This is fine – after all, it may not be essential to your research to know which town they grew up in nor would you be expected to know. It may however still be possible for you to research the subject of the interview rather than the person - for example, if you are interviewing one of the last survivors of the *Titanic*, you should find out everything you can about the *Titanic*.

When you have gathered as much information as you can within time limits and other constraints, spend a bit of time familiarising yourself with it. If you feel that some of the facts you have gathered may be particularly useful to raise during the course of the interview, commit them to memory or incorporate them into your questions (see the example about school above).

Recording sources of information

Whilst you are doing your research make a note of titles, authors and whereabouts of any publication you consult. File your notes in an index box for possible future reference.

Building your own sources

As your writing or researching career progresses, you will probably tend to specialise in certain subjects which you know most about. Many writers keep a special file of anything that is relevant to their area of expertise – newspaper cuttings, photocopies from journals and books, etc. In this way you build up your own best research sources.

Questions

Questions are the basic material of interviews. In practice, not only your questions but your body language and demeanour will also greatly influence what an interviewee will tell you and for more on body language see chapter 8, *Conducting the interview*. For the moment we shall look at how to get the best out of interviews by the questions we ask. The questions you ask will be dictated to a large extent by the demands of what you are going to write and the angle you have chosen.

Number of questions

There are no hard and fast rules for the number of questions you should ask in an interview and the most important consideration is that you ask the questions which will give you the copy you need. For a face-to-face interview lasting about an hour I usually find that between ten and fifteen main questions are enough. This does not mean that you will only ask ten or fifteen questions as sub questions will often grow out of the main question.

EXAMPLE

QUESTION: What led you to change your opinion so radically in 1975?
ANSWER: I went on a visit to Bangladesh.

QUESTION: What was it about Bangladesh that changed you?

In this case the interviewer did not know about the visit to Bangladesh (perhaps this is a case of poor research) but there was an obvious opening for another question.

How much someone is prepared to talk or not will also influence how many questions you ask. As a safeguard you may like to have a number of questions in reserve for the interviewee who can't seem to give an answer of more than three words.

Focusing

Before you even start to frame the questions, take a moment to form a clear idea in your own mind as to what you want from the interview. Sometimes it can help if you write this down quite specifically, e.g. 'To find out what life was really like for people working in the mines in the 1940s.' If you are writing an article, decide roughly how much time you want to spend focusing on each aspect. You would not want to spend a lot of time talking to a soccer star about his childhood if the main theme of your article is about how he relaxes after a game. Remind yourself again about what the magazine or paper wants. When you have a general idea of what you want to find out, break the idea down under separate headings. For the above example about working in the mines your headings may be:

Working conditions
Social life
Home life
View of the people working down the mines about what they were doing, etc.

Brainstorm and refine

Write down any questions that come to mind from each heading, no matter how stupid or trivial they may seem. This is just to get your mind working. You can discard any of them later but for the moment write down all of them. When you can't think of any more questions start to narrow them down to the most important ones, i.e. those which are relevant to your piece. Probably you will find some questions can be combined or are different ways of asking the same thing. Group your questions under the headings you have made.

Ordering the questions

Sometimes your questions will follow a natural order and at other times you will need to create an order. If you are tracing a biography or trying to reconstruct an event with someone, a chronological order helps to keep both you and the interviewee clear about what was going on where and when. Start at the beginning and finish close to the present. In some cases where you are trying to encourage someone to remember the past, you may find it appropriate to start at the nearest time and work backwards, but the principle of chronological order applies. Do not dive in and out of dates unless the person's memories are so hazy that a brainstorm approach seems more appropriate. For more on ordering questions see below under *Hints about asking questions* and chapter 8 under *Ad Libbing*.

Framing the questions

How you frame the questions can have a significant impact on the kinds of answers you receive. Consider the following questions:

- Does playing tennis help you unwind?
- Can you juggle being a mother and a top managing director easily?
- Is your ambition to play for England?
- Did people view work differently then?

The problem with asking questions like this is that they invite a mono-syllabic answer. Sometimes when asked a question like this, an interviewee may volunteer extra information (the answer to the second one might be 'No, I regularly feel like strangling my kids') but they might just say 'yes' or 'no', particularly if an interview is just getting under way and they are still nervous. In order to encourage people to talk you need to ask open-ended questions. These are questions which begin with the following:

Who?

What?

Where?

When?

Why?

How?

Asking interviewees 'What do you enjoy about writing?' gives them more scope to talk and to be both more detailed and more specific than if you had just asked 'Do you enjoy writing?' You can also easily follow up the first question with a sub-question 'What don't you like about it?' You may still get short answers from these kinds of questions, e.g., question: 'Why do you travel so much?', answer: 'I enjoy it' but you at least have a bit of meat to get your teeth into: 'What do you particularly enjoy?'

Hints about asking questions

- Always start with an easy opening question. Your interviewees needs to find their level and by starting off gently you are giving them the time to settle down and relax. The opening question can be fairly general and open-ended, e.g. 'How did you first get into politics/sky diving/ macramé?' Or you could use this time to gather in basic information that you have not been able to gather elsewhere, e.g. 'Could you just fill me in on a few basic facts about yourself – how long have you lived in this area?' (for more about starting the interview see chapter 8, *Conducting the interview*).
- If you are asking potentially sensitive questions, wait until the interviewees have settled down and are starting to feel relaxed with you.
- Try to end on a positive forward-looking note: 'What are your plans for the future of the gas works?'
- Make sure that your questions are clear and to the point. Do not use long sentences with endless sub-clauses containing several questions. Avoid questions like: 'What do you consider, given your previous

experience, to be the most important aspect or facet of working with the public, or at least working in the public domain and how do you go about ensuring that all your staff, at all levels, are aware of its importance – I mean has there ever been any occasion when you felt that your staff's needs were more important than the public's?'

- Do not tell your interviewees or suggest what you think the answer to the question is, e.g. 'You'd really like to be a success, wouldn't you?' It's not your job to tell the interviewees what they would like to be, it's their job to tell you.
- Pitch questions at an appropriate level. This may sound obvious but sometimes factors about your interviewee may influence the questions you ask. Age, level of education and socio-economic background need to be taken into account when you frame the question. If you are interviewing children, you should ask them in a language that they understand. Equally if you are interviewing elderly people, you need to respect their age without being patronising. You may not always know exactly what to expect beforehand and this can necessitate a certain amount of adjustment on your part, but be prepared to be flexible.

Writing down the questions

When you have framed and ordered your questions to your satisfaction, write them down in your notebook. Unless you are either totally confident or have total recall, you will need to take your questions with you. You can dispense with the notebook later in your career when you've dispensed with nerves. If you are intending to record the answers in the notebook, you will need to make sure that there is an adequate gap between answers for recording the information. I find it helpful to leave a full blank sheet between each question when I am recording manually as this gives me extra space for any overspill.

Other preparations – or neurotic musts

When you are at the interview there is no going back, no time to go and buy new batteries because your tape-recording machine has just ground to a halt, no time to go back home and pick up the camera you've forgotten and no time to wish the floor would swallow you up because you've left home with the wrong notepad and all your questions are sitting on the kitchen table. No time and no excuse. Before going to an interview, and preferably on the day before the interview, is when you should make sure that you have got everything ready. Make out a check list of everything you need to do. Here is a sample one:

- Buy new tapes and batteries for tape recorder (always take more than you need – tapes get chewed up and batteries can be faulty or run out if they are accidentally left on overnight). Take your tape recorder with you.
- If you are writing down notes take at least three ball-point pens (fountain pens leak and pencils don't look very professional). Take your notepad containing the questions with you.

- Make sure you have batteries and a film for your camera. Take your camera with you.
- Check petrol levels in car/travel arrangements and formulate contingency plans where possible.
- Check the address on a map so that you know exactly where you are going. Take the map with you.
- Make a copy of your interviewee's name and address and phone number to take with you.
- Buy a phone card and have small change available (in case you are late or lost and need to phone). If you have a mobile phone take it with you.

Err on the side of neurotic with interview preparation – it pays off.

Dress appropriately

Overdressing can make interviewees feel uncomfortable (not to mention the effects of high heels or stiff collars on you), underdressing creates an impression that you are either unprofessional or don't care and possibly both. Very often you will be meeting someone for the first time and you will want to create a professional impression, so it is better to dress up rather than down. Wear something that you feel comfortable in and that makes you feel good – this will boost your confidence. Forget the popular image of the journalist in a crumpled suit with beer stains down his shabby raincoat – leave that to the professionals who may be chasing after several interviews in a day. Give some thought to where you are going beforehand – stilettoes are not very well adapted to going down a mine, on an oil rig or across a muddy field, and a suit and tie would look rather out of place at a night-shelter for homeless people, so use your discretion. Use a briefcase or appropriate shoulder bag for carrying your tape recorder, camera and notepad, etc.

7
PSYCHING UP

You're nearly there. You've arranged your interview and your market, you've done as much preparation as you can, you've taken every possible precaution against things going wrong and now you're probably terrified. Welcome to the club. Anxiety about interviewing is endemic amongst new interviewers and this is as true of students on professional journalism courses as it is of the solitary freelance writer. I have yet to meet anyone who did not quake even just a little before the first interview. Many people quake for several interviews afterwards and it is only through practice that you reach a point where you do not quake at all.

In the next chapter we will look at ways in which you can help your interviewees overcome their fears but first we'll look at ways of overcoming your fears.

Why the fear?

In a real live interview situation you are completely on your own. No one is going to tell you how to do it nor are they going to step in and bail you out if it goes wrong. Equally no one is going to give you feedback afterwards about what you did well or suggest how you could have done it differently. The success or failure of the interview is entirely down to you and, if you have not interviewed before, this is quite a daunting prospect. On top of this you may be interviewing someone who is well known/very talented/essential/rich. Even if they are none of these, your interviewees are still important to you in terms of how they can help your writing or research. If you are new to interviewing you have the added anxieties of not knowing quite what to expect or how you will perform in a real live situation. No wonder it can all seem a little overwhelming.

Shooting down fantasies

If you are a beginner you will doubtless have a number of fantasies about interviewing and interviewees and some of these may be less than helpful. Below are some common ones and the facts with which to shoot them down:

Only professionals interview

Writing is so badly paid that many freelancers could not do it full time even if they wanted to. Many people write as a hobby or as a way of giving a framework to their particular interest – local historians collating information and putting it into a readable form, for instance. You do not have to be a full-time staff journalist on one of the daily broadsheets to go out and interview. The need to interview is dictated by the nature of the project, not by which publication you are writing for or how much you are being paid.

Why should they talk to me?
The answer is because you are the person who wants to ask them the questions. They are not obliged to talk to you but this does not take away your right to ask for an interview. If they have agreed to give you an interview, they have agreed to talk to you.

My publication isn't important
Let them decide on that. In practice most people are so flattered to be asked that they won't mind if your publication is the parish magazine or the *New York Times*. Having a big-name publication to write for can in fact be quite intimidating to your interviewee. Many people interview without having any intention of publishing the interview – genealogists and academic researchers might be amongst these .

I'm not important
You don't have to be 'important' (whatever that means) to interview. You are there to do a job; the important thing is that you are capable of doing the job.

I'm scared of getting it wrong/making a mess of it
No one can ever guarantee that things will go exactly right. The most you can do is follow basic guidelines and use common sense. Ninety-nine times out of a hundred these will be sufficient. It is very rare for an interview to be a complete unmitigated disaster and this will usually be the result of inadequate preparation which is the part over which you have some control.

I'm scared I'll seize up and forget what to say
In practice there is far more danger that your interviewee will seize up than you will (for more on this see under *Over-anxious interviewees* in chapter 10, *Trouble shooting*). If you have your notepad and questions with you there is no reason why you should seize up – you have what you need written down.

If you have any other fears and fantasies about interviewing try to analyse them rationally – you will usually find that the problem is more likely to originate in your head than in the reality of the situation.

The positive approach
No one can entirely remove all your fears about interviewing – this can be done only by going out and practising until you feel really confident – but below are a number of factors to consider which may help to counterbalance your anxieties:

Anxiety is what makes you good!
Actors often find that the real spur to their acting is the anxiety and stage fright they suffered beforehand. Without stress or tension we might never do anything. Anxiety is what makes you go the third mile in your preparations, what makes you take the trouble to do it as best you can and what will encourage you to do an even better interview next time.

Setting realistic expectations

If possible try to do your first few interviews with people who do not make you feel intimidated at the mere mention of their name. Often a friend, relative or someone you know will be a good choice. If you do have to interview a big name or a high flyer for your first interview, you will at least have got the worst over with and your successive interviews will seem comparatively easy. Do not think that you have to be a David Frost/Robin Day/Lynn Barber or Jeremy Paxman from Day One. Interviewing is as much a craft as it is an art and you have to learn the craft before you can start to develop it into an art. Unless you are very confident, do not start off trying to get the scoop of the century because your chances are minimal. Aim initially to do a competent job. 'Competent' here just means getting the answers you need for the questions you ask.

You are not alone

If you find yourself trying to pluck up courage to knock on someone's door or having a sleepless night because of worrying about tomorrow's interview, remember that virtually every interviewer has gone through or will go through the same process at some stage. Whilst this might not stop the worrying, it is a reminder that what you are feeling is perfectly natural and not a reflection on your unsuitability for interviewing.

Concentrate on the benefits

You are doing this interview for a purpose whether it is for money, work, information, help or status. Try to see the interview as a means to this end. Interviewing is a tool for helping you to get what you want, not an end in itself.

They want you to like them

As a writer you are in a powerful position. For most people who do not write, writers have a peculiar mystique. Mention that you are a writer and many people will automatically assume that you live on a higher planet. Whilst this is of course not the case – writers get stuck in queues at supermarkets as much as the next person – and I am certainly not suggesting that you try to trade off other people's assumptions, it is often helpful to bear in mind that you automatically assume a lot of credibility in other people's eyes simply by virtue of what you are doing. In other words, your job will create a good impression for you and your interviewee will probably be quite keen to impress you. Moreover, in the cases where the interview will appear in a wide-reaching publication such as a magazine or in an enduring one such as a book, few people are going to want to appear at anything other than their best. It is not unusual to be given the red-carpet treatment when you are a writer. Accept it graciously and enjoy it – it's one of the perks.

Mutual benefits

Interviews very often serve the interests of both the interviewer and the interviewee. In some cases your writing may be promoting a product or company, it will certainly be advertising them. Other possible benefits for the interviewee include acknowledging a person's professional status or expertise. Many people find the fact that someone wants to interview them extremely flattering and exciting. Some people may just be grateful that someone is genuinely interested in what they have to say – elderly people who may be living alone could fall into this category. Given half a chance most people like to talk about themselves and what they hold dear to them. In the rush of modern life few people are given the luxury of the whole-hearted attention of an interested and informed listener who will give them a whole hour or more free. Unless your intention is to dig out the dirt, the chances are that they will get as much, if not more, out of the interview as you do and you may find your problem will be actually managing to get away at the end. Don't forget that your interviewees could actually feel far more indebted to you than you do to them.

Professionalism

When you interview someone for your writing you usually do so in a professional role – as a writer, journalist or researcher, for example. Even if you are interviewing purely for your own interest – as an amateur local historian or a genealogist, for example – you are engaged on a serious project of research and you should approach it in a professional spirit. Whether you are interviewing the prime minister or a prize-marrow grower you need to remember that you are doing a job. You have a set task to ask questions and to record answers. The person's status is of secondary importance. Your duty when doing interviews is to your publication or project. If it helps, think of yourself as doing the interview for someone else (your editor, for example, or for the work you are trying to produce) rather than for you. This takes some of the pressure off you.

It's worse for them

Interviewees take a big risk when they agree to talk to you. They can risk exposing themselves to the scrutiny of literally thousands of people. They do not know you or exactly what your intentions are. Being interviewed is a far more risky business than interviewing. You as the interviewer are calling the shots and are in the position of power – no matter how bad it is for you it is likely to be worse for them. Even the great and good can feel anxious before an interviewer – even a novice.

Enjoy it

Interviews can provide some of their most interesting experiences with some of the most interesting people. You have the opportunity to drop briefly into people's lives and find out more about them than would probably be possible if you had known them for a number of years. Interviewers are in a very privileged position – enjoy it.

Your attitude

It takes courage to go out and interview someone. Don't berate yourself for your fear or trepidation. Congratulate yourself for having got this far and for having the courage to go ahead with it.

Supportive measures
Practice
Practice, they say, makes perfect. Even if it doesn't it can help considerably. If you are very new to interviewing, not sure what to expect, or are uncertain about which button to press on your tape recorder, try running through your questions with a willing spouse or friend. If you can't find one there's always the cat or a mirror. Practice will give you a feel for the interview and help you anticipate what may actually arise during the real thing. Try changing places with your friend so that you get some idea of what it's like to be in the interviewee's shoes as well.

If you are very nervous the following may help:
- Bach Flower Rescue Remedy.
- Relaxation exercises, meditation or yoga.
- The thought of a pay cheque.
- The thought of the editor's wrath if you don't do it (it may be worse than the fear of the interview).
- The thought that your friends will be impressed.

In extremis
- A stiff drink (one only).
- Take part in a dangerous sport beforehand – it will help put everything in perspective and also help you work off some anxiety.
- Take a large bet with someone who says that you won't go ahead with it.
- Send someone in your place.

Afterwards
Plan to give yourself a reward when you finish the interview. Whether it's a cup of cappuccino, a night watching videos or a weekend break in Paris, make sure that you have something to look forward to afterwards.

8
CONDUCTING
THE INTERVIEW

Face-to-face interviews

All your previous preparation has been building up to this point and, provided you have the right time, date, place, equipment and person, you are now ready to do the interview itself. Because you are dealing with people in an interview situation you will find that no two interviews are exactly the same and you can never predict exactly how an interview is going to proceed and what information you will gain from it. What follows is therefore a guideline as to what to expect in a one-to-one face to face interview but it is not a formula. For variants in interviews see chapter 8, *In the event of. . .*

Arriving

The golden rule is arrive a little early. If you arrive in the area with plenty of time, you can avoid becoming panic stricken before you even walk through the door. Being early does not mean that you have to be hours ahead of schedule but allow yourself sufficient time to find out exactly where you are supposed to go. If you have any spare time you can use it to walk round the block noting your surroundings (this may be useful later on when you come to write up your piece), and to take a few minutes to collect yourself, run through your questions again, breathe deeply to steady your nerves and focus on the forthcoming interview. You should always aim to be on time for an interview itself. Avoid being early and avoid being late. If you need to find your interviewee via a secretary, you may want to allow a few extra minutes for this.

When you meet your interviewee smile and shake hands (where appropriate) – first impressions are important. It is often helpful to briefly remind your interviewee who you are and your purpose, e.g. 'I'm Ann Author, I rang you last week to arrange to have a talk about your role in Amnesty International for a book I'm writing on prisoners of conscience.' Some interviewees will need no reminding of why you have come and may have been anxiously awaiting you all week, especially if the outcome of the interview is particularly important to them. Others, people who are very busy, very popular or very used to being interviewed, may not have you at the forefront of their mind.

The niceties

There may be some preliminary niceties to go through before the interview starts, such as discussing the weather or your journey there or being offered a cup of coffee. This is all well and good and is a helpful way of breaking the ice. Don't launch straight into your questions until you and your interviewee are sitting down and are reasonably settled.

Putting them at their ease

Try to use this time to set up a rapport with your interviewees. Your interviewees may be a little nervous, suspicious or they may even be terrified. Even the rich and famous are not immune to interview nerves. The best way of making them feel confident is to act in a relaxed friendly way yourself. Try sitting back in your chair, smile, relax and, where appropriate, comment on something other than the approaching interview – admire the garden or the view or a picture on the wall, stroke the dog, ask if they've lived there long. If you sense that some one is extremely nervous, it can sometimes be helpful to refer to your own shortcomings, e.g. 'It's a while since I last did an interview like this, I feel slightly out of practice' (even if this is not true it does put you in a human light). If you feel it is appropriate, address people by their first name but use your discretion on this one. Many people find that there is something very appealing about being addressed by their first name but be careful of assuming over-familiarity, in particular with interviewees who are much older than yourself and people in a professional position. If someone has a title (doctor, professor, etc.) it is a mark of respect to use it. As an interviewer your position is akin to that of a guest in someone's house – good manners, courtesy and respect are all important and remember that your interviewee is a fellow human being, not just a source of information. For more on anxious interviewees see under chapter 10, *Trouble shooting*.

Taking control

Do not let the initial niceties drag on to the point where they grind to an awkward silence. Always remember that you are there to do a job and your interviewee may have a thousand and one other things to do. You should also bear in mind that because of nerves your interviewee may actually want to put off the moment when the interview starts so, when there is an appropriate lull in the conversation, you should take charge. A good way of doing this is to take out your recorder or notebook and say something like: 'As I said on the phone, I'd like to talk to you today about your business sales/latest album/compost heap. . .' Taking control is an essential part of good interviewing. The idea of controlling the interview may seem a little strange, particularly if you are new to interviewing or are sitting opposite a Nobel Prize winner or your favourite rock star, but remember that you are not an awed member of the public when you interview; you are a professional and you are meeting someone on professional terms. If you believe this your interviewee will also believe it. Taking control does not mean being pushy or overbearing or domineering; it simply means being directive, i.e. starting the interview, making sure that you ask all your questions and finishing appropriately. Your interviewees will take their cue from you. They will be expecting to meet a competent interviewer who will ask questions which they will answer. If you dither around or do not seem to know what to do next, your interviewee will lose confidence in you. In some ways it is like playing a role. No matter how anxious you are, you must act as if you are confident and in control – if you can assume this role the rest is likely to follow smoothly.

NOTE This does not mean that you should not behave in a rather bumbling way with the sole intention of putting your interviewee more at their ease if you deem it to be appropriate, but this should be through choice and at your discretion, not through disorganisation on your part.

Explaining the process

As you are about to begin the interview you may find it beneficial to explain to your interviewee what you are intending to do. This gives them some idea of what is expected of them which in turn can help reduce anxiety. Say something like 'I'm mainly interested in talking to you about . . . I'd just like to go through about ten questions with you. . .' If someone has probably not been interviewed before or is quite young I always ask them: 'Have you ever done an interview before?' If they say 'no' I explain the process briefly, pointing out that it doesn't matter if they don't get it exactly right, or if all the answers do not come out in perfectly formulated sentences and ideas, because I will be editing their replies into good English before I complete the work. Sometimes it is also helpful to point out that no two interviews are ever identical, so there is no right and wrong way of being interviewed.

Use of tape recorder

Always ask if they mind you using a tape recorder. Some people really are unable to function when there is one in front of them but most will go along with it. It is often helpful to ask as if you are assuming that they will not mind and you are merely being polite, for example: 'Is it alright if I use this – my shorthand's pretty rusty these days'. People are less likely to refuse that way and in any case most people will forget about the tape recorder, once the interview is properly under way. Try to place the tape recorder equidistant from you and your interviewee – on the desk or a coffee table or even on a window sill. It is best not to have it in too obtrusive a position. I usually do a quick trial run to see if it is picking up from where I have placed it by saying what the tape is about and what the date is (e.g. 'Interview with Sonia Sheldon for *Life Span* magazine, 31 March 1995') and then I play it back. When you are sure that the recorder is picking up you are ready to begin.

Techniques to use in the interview

Once your interview is under way the rest should be a fairly straightforward matter of asking the questions and recording the answers but, until you actually do the interview, you can never be quite sure what kinds of answers you are going to get to your questions. Below are a few suggestions of ways of getting the most from your interviewee.

Asking questions

If you have ordered your questions carefully you should begin with an easy general one that allows people time to find their feet. You could also start by filling in on basic information that you have not been able to obtain in the course of your research: 'How many cats did you say you had?' Don't be surprised if their answer is short – people often need to warm to their subject.

Once you have started the rest should follow. You have a clear remit to ask the questions and record the answers. Keep your questions on your lap where you can easily refer to them but don't be too eager to move on to the next question. Sometimes a little prompting from you can elicit further information. The following are useful in encouraging your interviewee to expand on what they are saying:

Body language Nodding, smiling and other facial expressions can all indicate that you are following what is being said and taking an interest. The extent to which you can influence someone by your body language is hard to measure but quite considerable. Equally by being ready to read your interviewees' body language you can adapt your style appropriately to get the best out of them. If they are sitting on the edge of their seat with their arms tightly folded, their breathing is shallow and they are not smiling, they are probably highly anxious. If you can relax back in your seat, smile and speak in a calm, friendly way, your interviewees are likely to relax more too. When interviewing give people your attention but do not fix your gaze on them – it is both intimidating and irritating. Maintain sufficient eye contact so that it feels comfortable but look away at regular intervals too. If you are taking down the interview by hand, try not to lose eye contact for longer than is necessary – with practice you should be able to write by just using peripheral vision which will enable you to see the page out of the corner of your eye whilst you still manage to retain facial contact with the interviewee.

Prompters Your responses to what is said can encourage someone to go on and say more. As well as nodding, saying 'mmm' or 'really?' or repeating back what someone has said or asking a relevant question ('you didn't like it when he said that, then?') can all encourage people to expand on what they are saying. Doing this can be quite hard work and you need to guard against the possibility of sounding false or patronising but, if you are genuinely interested in what is being said, this should not be a problem. In many ways good interviewing skills are akin to the listening skills involved in counselling, although in interviewing you need to be directive.

Silence It may seem surprising but silences can actually be very productive in an interview. This is because most people feel quite uncomfortable with silence, especially if they are with a stranger. Instead of rushing on to the next question as soon as there is a lull in your interviewee's speech, wait a few seconds and nod and smile expectantly. Your interviewees may take this as a cue to go on talking and in any case the silence may make them feel that they want to.

Listen! Always try to give the impression that you are listening to what is being said – even if you are not particularly interested or your interviewee talks in an uninspiring or rambling fashion. Do not look at your watch, yawn, let your attention or gaze wander, and always try to respond appropriately to what is being said. As a beginner you may have the opposite problem and find that you are not listening because you are over concerned with doing the interview correctly and getting the information down. Be aware of this happening and allow yourself a little time to relax into the interview.

Ad-libbing If you are new to interviewing you may not be confident enough to deviate from the order in which you have written your questions but, as you progress, you will see that your questions are there only as an aid and a prompt. Creative interviewing is not about sticking to a rigid agenda and, if it seems more appropriate to ask a later question at an earlier stage because your interviewee has already raised the subject, be prepared to do so.

In your anxiety to get through the questions you may miss out on potentially useful material. Whilst answering a question your interviewee may refer in passing to something that is of possible interest but does not fit in with your line of questions, for example: 'I took up sky diving in 1983 – shortly after I came out of hospital.' Whilst the next question in your notepad might be 'Where did you do your first sky dive?', put this on hold for a moment – there may be some mileage in asking 'Why were you in hospital?'

Do not become hypnotised by the order or number of questions that you have formulated. Be prepared to go with an interesting line of questioning – this is where discoveries lie.

Exploring

Sometimes your interviewees say something which sounds quite interesting ('Of course, Robbie was always the brains behind the operation. . .') but then go silent. In this case you may want them to tell you more so you need to explore the issue. There is a story here but you need to bring it out and to do this you will have to be persistent. Useful phrases might be:
- Could you tell me a bit more about that?
- That sounds really interesting – can we look at it in a bit more detail?
- Can you explain that to me?
- Why do you think that is?

Clarifying

When you are not quite sure what your interviewee is trying to say, you need to clarify it. The following phrases (and any similar ones) buy you some time before your interviewee moves on:
- Can I just check that I've understood that correctly. Are you saying. . .?
- Do you mean that. . .?
- So would it be true to say that. . .?

Summarising

Summarising is similar to clarifying but is primarily used if your interviewees are long-winded, tend to ramble or are speaking about complex matters and you need to tie up the loose ends. Summarising is also a way of indicating to them that you have been listening and are interested in what they are saying and is a way for you to check that you have got your facts right:

- So, as I understand it. . .
- Let's see what we've got then. . .
- That's quite important, perhaps it would be helpful if I ran over what you've just said and you can tell me if I've got it right. . .

Devil's advocate

In playing devil's advocate you test a proposition by putting the opposite case, even though it may not be your own point of view. This approach is often seen on TV interviews when the interviewer uses the technique in a direct and forceful way, for instance, using the Opposition's more extreme arguments to provoke a government minister into unscripted comments. This approach can often yield useful copy but is not for the faint-hearted. A less direct way to disagree with them without involving yourself, to raise a controversial issue or draw out an opinion, is to use phrases such as:

- Some people might say that...
- There is an argument that. . .
- What would you say if. . .

Sensitive questions

It is probably not a good idea to start off your interviewing career by doing interviews which involve probing deeply into someone's private and personal life but sometimes these are unavoidable. Here are a few guidelines. Do not ask a potentially sensitive or delicate question until the interview is well under way. Part of the reason for this is that your interviewee may want to call a halt to the interview there and then and you need to make sure that you have already got sufficient information to write your piece. The other part of the reason is that it is unrealistic (and potentially rude and insensitive) to expect people to answer a difficult question when they have only just met you ('Hallo, I'd like to ask you about your recent court appearance on a drugs charge.') When you have built up a rapport with subjects, they become more willing to open up to you, but how you eventually ask the question is down to your discretion. Sometimes it might feel more appropriate to hedge around the issue: 'What are your feelings about the legalisation of drugs?' and gradually steer the questioning round to the interviewees' own experience. At other times a more direct approach might seem better: 'Has your recent court experience altered the way you view recreational drugs at all?' You will probably notice a change in body language when you have asked a potentially difficult question. Note it both for your future piece and to gauge how the subjects are responding to your questions. Remain detached and courteous. If they refuse to talk about it there is nothing you can do to force them, other than suggest something like: 'Obviously it's up to you whether you want to discuss it but I think it may be helpful if we could both set the record straight on paper. . .'

Incisive questions

An occasion may arise in the course of the interview when an opportunity to ask a burning and potentially awkward question is offered to you on a plate.

EXAMPLE: your interviewee who is rumoured to be very well endowed with money, but who pays his staff at the rate of a pound an hour, muses to himself 'People must think I'm made of money'. The question to ask is 'Well aren't you?'

Incisive questions are short and to the point (Are you? Do you? Is it?) but do not say them in such a way as to put your interviewees on their guard. Ask as if you are genuinely interested and sometimes it might be appropriate to introduce a note of humour. Your interviewee may laugh off your question but even that can be potentially useful ('"Of course I'm not made of money," he said, looking out through the window towards his two-hundred-acre estate.').

Quotable quotes

Most kinds of writing benefit from lively quotes or paraphrases (except perhaps scientific theses). Good journalism relies heavily on quotable quotes. When you are new to interviewing you do not need to be over concerned about getting a good quote but as you become more experienced you should keep an ear open for the following:

The surprising quote Supermum Madonna Mummery said 'I never thought I'd want kids when I was growing up.'

The witty quote 'After all that drinking I needed to get some blood into my alcohol stream.'

The revealing quote From a famous actor: 'Of course, it's lonely at the top but it's even more lonely when you're back on the way down.'

Anecdotes

Like a good quote, anecdotes about funny, sad, revealing or whimsical incidents can breathe life into your piece. Sometimes your interviewee may tell you a few in the course of the interview but you can also try to extract a few if you feel they would be useful for your writing. You can ask directly by saying something like 'Do you remember any good anecdotes from your days in the army?' or try to draw out a story if you sense that one is in the offing.

Keeping on track

Whilst your biggest fear may be that you will get an interviewee who has nothing to say, the opposite could happen and you may find yourself interviewing someone who has too much to say of which only a small amount is relevant. People can ramble and go off at tangents in interviews for various reasons – some people are just naturally prone to doing that, others may be doing it because they are nervous or have forgotten what you asked them; sometimes it is because they are trying to avoid the question. If you find that they have gone off the point, try tactfully to bring them back. Smile, nod and at the first appropriate pause and say something like: 'Going back to the question of how you first got involved in working for the Mafia, are you saying that it more or less came about by accident?' or, 'Can I just clarify with you that you became involved in the Mafia because. . .'

Personal opinions

During the course of the interview your interviewees may express opinions that you strongly disagree with or strongly endorse. As a general rule it is not a good idea to get too involved or drawn into an argument or discussion. You are not, after all, there to talk about what you think – you want to find out about what they think. You can always challenge their views by playing devil's advocate and saying something like: 'Some people might say that unemployment is an economic problem, not a result of laziness on the part of the unemployed. . . what do you think about that view?,' but avoid getting personal. There is no rule in interviewing that says you have to agree with what is said. You may find that if you start to tell your interviewees what you think that they clam up altogether. You may also find yourself being shown the door if you openly disagree with them. Always stay detached.

Self-disclosure

In most conversations there is a bit of give and take with both participants talking about themselves in turn. In an interview your position is different. No matter how relaxed and friendly the interview is or how much you find yourself enjoying it, do not forget that you want the interviewees to talk about themselves, not you to talk about yourself. Whilst a certain amount of self-disclosure may be helpful in breaking the ice ('I could never be a mountaineer like you – I'm so scared of heights I need crampons to climb up the staircase'), illustrating a question (I know from my own experience that travelling alone with children can be a nightmare – how do you manage to do it so often with twenty?') and showing your interviewees that you understand what they say ('Yes, I know what you mean when you say that the hardest part of being burgled is the thought that someone has actually been inside your own home – that's exactly how we felt when our house was broken in to'), your disclosures should be for the benefit of the interview, not an opportunity for a chat or as a platform for you and your views.

Use of sympathy

If someone tells you something difficult or painful or if your interview necessitates that you ask about difficult painful areas such as divorce, bereavement and failure, aim to be sympathetic but do not get too drawn into what they are saying. You are not there as a social worker or counsellor and, whilst you can be sympathetic, you should also be non-committal. You can follow up what they say with something like: 'That must have been really difficult for you,' or 'You seem to have coped very well inspite of everything.' Very often sympathy will encourage your subject to open up more to you but you should always maintain a degree of detachment from the situation. Your ultimate loyalties are to your publication.

The uses of ignorance

If you have done your research properly you should have a fairly good idea of what your interviewees are talking about and, indeed, there may be occasions when you find that you know more about the subject than they do (assuming this is not a profile piece where they are talking about themselves). If you want to encourage someone to talk, it is not a good idea to keep interrupting with what you know about the subject. If the interviewees sense that you are better informed than they are, it will inhibit them. Particularly if you are dealing with an ordinary member of the public, treat your interviewees as if they are the expert – listen with respect, show interest and let them feel as if they are teaching you something. No matter how much factual knowledge you have, there is no real substitute for talking to someone who has first-hand knowledge.

Place

As well as noting your external surroundings (see above under arriving), you may find that for some interviews it will be useful to take note of the place in which you are sitting. Journalists in particular may want a little local colour to spice up their piece, but other writers and researchers, such as people researching a biography *in situ*, a local history project or an historical novel, may find that there is as much to gain from noting the decor and toilet-roll holders in a setting as there is from talking to the interviewee. If the building you are in is particularly noteworthy or in some way relevant to what you are writing (e.g. a piece about the only white-chocolate factory in the country), you will often be given a guided tour as a matter of course. People who live in beautiful houses usually like to show them off and, if it is appropriate, you may want to ask to be shown something of specific interest ('Would it be possible to look at the maze in your garden after the interview?').

Even if the place where the interview is taking place is not very important, you can add a lot to your writing just by noting the overall effect of your immediate surroundings. Be prepared to make mental notes about the decor – was it luxurious/austere/psychedelic? Journalists are often advised to ask to use the bathroom before they leave to get a better impression of the surroundings. Quite what amazing revelations they expect to find there remains something of a mystery although once in a very long while you may find someone has pinned up all their bad reviews, rejection slips or Ph.D. certificate in the lavatory.

For more on this see under chapter 11, *Transcribing and writing up*.

People watching

You may gain useful material and anecdotes from what your interviewees are doing as well as what they are saying. This type of information is particularly useful for profile features but can be extended to other kinds of writing too. A captain of industry playing nervously with executive toys, or reaching for cigarettes whilst talking about the future prospects of his company, may be saying something. You can always leave it up to your reader to work out what ('Bob Bigbucks fumbled for his cigarettes as he spoke with glowing praise about how well the company was doing'). Use your discretion on this one – don't let your interviewees think that you are watching every move they make and making a note of it – write it down discreetly or mentally store it to be recorded later. If there are any other people (including children) or animals around, you may be able to glean something useful just by observing interactions (e.g. the fact that supermum and actress Sibyl Sparkle spoke more to her plants than to her children). I once gained some very useful copy for an article I was writing by listening to a conversation between an author and his dog. The name of the dog was important in this case too as it shed some light on a story the author had written.

Concluding

You can give your interviewees forewarning that the interview is nearly finished by saying: 'My last question is. . .' or ' One last question before we finish. . .' You can always ask your interviewee after your last question whether they can think of anything else to add that might be useful. Conclude the interview by smiling and saying something like: 'I think that's all I need to know/ask. Thank you very much – this has been really helpful'. Even if what you have heard has not been particularly useful, tell them that it has – they have done you a favour by giving you their time. Before you finish off go through anything you are not totally sure of and check that you know how to spell their name correctly. I always ask if I can get in touch if I think of something that I forgot to ask in the interview, but this is really only a safety net and not something I ever normally do. For most people, being rung after the event does not present a problem but some people are very busy and may not appreciate you taking much more of their time. If you are writing a piece for a newspaper or magazine and are a freelance journalist, your interview may well have sparked off ideas for other markets and you could ask at this point if they would be willing to be interviewed again for another piece - if you are promoting them they will usually be very happy to oblige and equally, if the interview has been a courteous and pleasant one, they should not have any objection. You will probably find anyway that you have more material from just the one interview than you can use in one piece of writing and you could inform them at this stage that you would like to use the interview for other publications. Most people won't mind but, understandably, may like to be kept informed as to where their name is going to turn up in print.

Gather together your things and put them in your bag, but don't switch off your mind as you switch off your tape recorder. You can gain a surprising amount of information from someone when the formal interview has finished. Often it is at this point that your interviewees truly begin to relax and unwind (either because the interview is over or because it hasn't been as bad as they feared it might be) and so you can get a glimpse of them really being themselves. They may now offer to show you around or reveal something that they did not say in the interview. Obviously you don't want to get out your biro or tape recorder again but store up any gems in your memory and write them down as soon as you reasonably can when you have left.

Photos

If you need a photo of your interviewee (or something connected with them), leave it to the end when your interviewee will be much more relaxed. When you have finished asking your questions just ask 'Can I take a photo now?' Many people associate photographs with interviews so this should not come as too much of a surprise, or you may have already mentioned that you would like a photo when you set up the interview. Always take more than one photo – preferably with two cameras. For articles in particular photographs can be very important and this is something you want to get right. Make sure that your interviewee is in a relaxed natural position with anything highly relevant in view where possible (such as a bravery award or ancestral portraits). Avoid obvious photographic mistakes like plants seeming to grow out of your interviewee's head. If the publication you are writing for has a staff photographer, let your interviewees know before you leave that they are likely to be approached: 'They will probably want a photo to go with this piece so they should be in touch when they are getting it ready for publication.' Sometimes you could ask your interviewee to supply a photo – particularly if you are doing something promotional – which could save on your costs.

'When will it be out?'

Even the rich and famous quite like to know when their name will be in print – if only to add to their scrapbook collection. If you are writing a book you may have a rough idea of when it will be published. For freelance journalists dates of publication can be more difficult to gauge. Some editors will have your piece in the next edition after you've submitted it and others might hang on to it for months. If you don't know, give a general idea ('I think the Editor will try to include it in the March edition but it depends on space, so I'd keep a look out for it around that time'). If you haven't got a firm commission, say which publication it is likely to appear in ('The editor of *Reebok World* was definitely interested. . .') and let them look out for it.

Telephone interviewing

What preceded was a rundown of what to do in a face to face interview session. You will sometimes find that it is easier, more convenient or just more sensible to do your interview over the phone. (For knowing when to do a telephone interview, see chapter 2, *Methods of interviewing* and *Types of interview*).

A telephone interview is generally much simpler to arrange than a face-to-face interview. You don't have to worry about the practical considerations of being in the right place at the right time with the right person and nor do you have to worry about the 'neurotic musts' outlined in chapter 6. None the less, interviewing by phone carries its own stresses and below is an outline of what to expect and how to be best prepared for them.

Contacting the interviewee

The important point to remember when interviewing by phone is that you may manage to speak to your intended interviewee as soon as you ring up, so it is essential that you have your questions ready prepared and a means of recording them ready to hand.

If you are ringing up the press office (see chapter 5, *Getting the interview*), you will probably find someone ready to talk to you there and then (after all, it is the press officer's job to answer questions posed by people like yourself). If you are ringing to talk to specific experts, you will probably have to contact them via a secretary. Sometimes you will be put through straight away and at other times you may be asked to ring later or be told that the person you want to speak to will ring you back. At other times you may find yourself talking directly to the person you need. If you are not sure whom you want to talk to, ask if there is anyone available who might be suitable – for a charity agency for example: 'I'm particularly interested in talking to someone who has had recent experience of working in a hospital in the war zone'.

When you have tracked down the person you need to talk to, say who you are and why you are ringing ('I'm Harry Hack and I'm researching a piece for the *Daily Chronicle* on. . . I wondered if I could ask you a few questions about. . .'). It's often a good idea to check that you are ringing at a convenient time ('Is it all right to talk at the moment or would you prefer it if I rang back at a more convenient time?'). Don't assume that people are not busy. If they have agreed to talk with you, but not at this exact moment, you can offer to ring back later or they may offer to ring you. If they are ringing you back from a business number, you do not have to worry too much about the costs they are incurring but other individuals should not have to bear the burden of the cost of a telephone call for an interview. If private individuals ring you back later, offer to ring them ('Let me ring you back, I should be paying for this'). If the conversation is likely to be a long one (and you cannot always predict that it won't be), try to ring during off-peak times where possible. Make sure that you have time for the phone call (it may be as long as half an hour or more because some people either like the sound of their own voice or have a great deal to tell you) and do not try to rush it.

Sometimes you may have no choice but to make your phone call from a public phone box (if you can only get someone at a certain time but cannot be near a private phone at the same time for instance). If this is the case, either have plenty of change (preferably larger rather than smaller denominations) or make sure you have plenty of units left on a phone card. The best solution is probably to carry a BT card which enables you to make calls from a phone box for any length of time, whilst the cost is charged to your home account.

Conducting the telephone interview

Assuming you have got the person you want to talk to on the other end of the line and he or she has agreed that now is a convenient time to talk, you can go ahead and ask your questions. As with a face-to-face interview it is important that you are in control. Keep your questions clear and to the point and do not get drawn into lengthy discussion. Unlike a face-to-face interview, you will have no visual cues as to how your interviewees are responding to your questions. If you are trying to get purely factual information or are more interested in the opinion of the subjects rather than in them as persons, this is not really important. However, you should be aware of the cues people are giving out by the tone of their voice. Most people who agree to be interviewed on the phone will give both their time and opinions fairly readily. You should be wary though of taking up too much of their time. Listen to see if they are sounding impatient, sighing or giving you short answers. Sometimes your subject matter may be the problem (this is particularly true for journalists who are dealing with sensitive issues – however, if your brief from the editor is to find out just why Company X is being investigated for fraud, you have no choice but to pursue the issue and presumably you have agreed to do some investigative journalism knowing that it will not always make you popular). You may occasionally have the dilemma of knowing that your interviewees are impatient to finish the interview but equally you need to get the information they can give you. If this is the case, it pays to be a little thick-skinned. Getting your information should be the priority.

When you have asked all your questions or received as much information as you can get, conclude the interview. As with face-to-face interviews you can finish by saying something like 'I think that's all I need to ask. Thank you very much for talking to me – it's been really helpful'. People like to be thanked and they like to feel that they have been of help to someone, so do not miss out on the niceties, even if, as with face-to-face interviews, you feel that the interview has not been particularly helpful. Before you ring off, make sure that you know how to spell the person's name – if you have only heard it on the phone it is easy to get it wrong – and what the work or personal title is where appropriate.

Recording information on the phone

In a telephone interview you have little choice but to record information by writing it down. Unfortunately, because the interviewee cannot see you doing this, he/she may not make any allowances for the fact that you are desperately trying to scribble down what is being said whilst also trying to sound interested. Pauses on the phone can seem more awkward than pauses when you are face to face with someone and you may feel under more pressure to keep the conversation flowing. There are no easy answers to this but the following may help:

- Keep your questions as simple as possible.
- Leave lots of space where you can scribble down your answer.
- If you cannot get the whole of it down, listen for the gist of what is being said.
- Play for time – repeat back what people have said and try to clarify it with them: 'So what you are saying is that. . .', 'Would it be true to say then that. . .', etc.
- Ask them to repeat it (but not too often): 'Sorry I didn't quite manage to get all of that down and it's really useful/interesting stuff, could you just tell me again'.
- At some point in the proceedings let them know that you are trying to write down what they are saying ('Sorry, I'm trying to write this leaning on the wall and my pen doesn't like being horizontal').

- Check anything you are unsure of with them at the end.
- Ask if you can contact them again if there is anything else you need to know. That gives you licence to ring back and check that you have got what they said right. It is in their interests as well as yours that what they say is recorded accurately.

Most people will be sympathetic. Some people will be so eager for you to get down every word that they will practically say it in slow motion.

Post–mortems

If you have done an interview as a one off and do not expect to ever have to interview again, you can congratulate yourself for having done it and go on to the writing-up stage. But let's hope the interview will have left you eager to do more, in which case it can often help to have a short post-mortem after your first few interviews. The sole benefit of a post-mortem is to help you to do a better job next time (even interviews which have gone extremely well can benefit from a short reflection on what it was that made them so good). There is nothing to be gained from simply looking at everything you felt you did wrong or concentrating exclusively on the embarrassing bits, even though human nature very often seems to compel us to do this. In a good post-mortem you make a rational assessment of how the interview went, what you thought were its strengths and weaknesses, and make a note of things to capitalise on (such as managing to remain flexible enough to ask relevant questions there and then rather than simply relying on the notes in front of you) and possible areas for improvement (such as rushing on to the next question without giving the interviewee time to expand on what they were saying).

Inevitably your first few interviews might not be quite as you would have liked them to be – good interviewing like everything else comes with time and practice – but don't set your sights too high initially. Because you are very much on your own in an interview situation, the finished product is the main yardstick with which to measure how well it went. If you managed to get the information you needed in sufficient amounts for you to write your piece, your interview has been good enough. If you enjoyed it (and most people do) that is an added bonus.

9
IN THE EVENT OF. . .

The previous chapter looked at ways of conducting a straightforward interview. In reality you will find that every interview is different because in most you will be dealing with a new person and asking different kinds of questions. No book could be comprehensive enough to cover all the permutations possible in an interview situation, but what follows is a look at some variations which you may expect to encounter at some point in your interviewing career.

Interviewing couples

In the classic interview situation the interviewer is alone with the interviewee but there are some occasions where you may find yourself interviewing two people who are both equally important to your interview – this could be husband and wife partnerships, business partners, ballet dancing duos, Siamese twins. . . The procedure is exactly the same and these kinds of interviews tend to go particularly well (the chance of there being awkward silences is reduced by 50 per cent for a start). People tend to be more confident with a partner and couples tend to bounce ideas off each other and spark off each other's memories. Interviews with couples often have an element of fun too because people are usually more relaxed.

One possible drawback that you should bear in mind is that most couples (of whatever nature) tend to have one partner who is more vociferous than the other. There is nothing wrong with this as long as you are getting the information you need but you may find when you come to write up your interview that a piece about two people is overloaded by quotes from one of them. This is particularly important for feature articles where the article can start to become rather unbalanced. Be aware of this during the interview and try to direct the conversation equally to both partners. If one person is talking all the time, a simple query: 'And what do you think about that, Mrs Smith?' will usually suffice.

Interviewing groups

This is probably not a good way to start off your interviewing career as it requires a considerable amount of verbal dexterity and a knowledge of group dynamics on your part, but you may at some point find it helpful to interview a group of people – a football team or pressure-campaign group, for example. Often if you are doing this kind of interview you are searching for a variety of opinions and it can be helpful to conduct the interview as if it were a discussion with you acting as chairperson. Remember to stay in charge and, if someone is talking all the time, direct the focus away from him or her by asking 'And what do the rest of you think?' You can ask people to give their names when they speak or ask for them afterwards, depending on which approach seems more appropriate.

Interviewing children

The show business adage of never work with children and animals doesn't apply to interviewers. Well, the children part of it doesn't. Children can provide a fruitful source of quotations which are often funny, sometimes poignant and occasionally surprising. There are times when interviewing children might be essential – if you are researching a thesis on children's changing reactions to children's fiction, for instance, you would probably want to consult some opinions from children in the relevant age group. At other times you might want to interview a local child prodigy or you may want to do a survey of what schoolchildren think of the latest change in the education curriculum.

Treat children as intelligent beings with a short attention span. Make the interview as pleasant and interesting for them as possible and keep your language at an appropriate level. Often an interview conducted on informal lines is best. Do not pressurise them to give you any answers. If you have children of your own, you have a ready made source of interviewees but, unless you are interviewing other children for a vox-pop, it is usual to consult with their parents or school beforehand. There are several restrictions on identifying children or juveniles (those under the age of 17) in connection with legal proceedings. For more on this and other legal matters for the press see *McNae's Essential Law for Journalists* (see *Booklist*).

Interviewing elderly people

Elderly people can be a wonderful source of material in particular for local historians or genealogists. Many elderly people love to talk about their pasts and, if they are retired, will often be able to give you a lot of interview time. Memories of old people are often more valuable for gaining impressions of life than for hard and fast facts. Given that most of us would probably find it difficult to remember what the weather was like last week, it would hardly be surprising if someone could not remember the exact date when a village hall opened fifty years ago and you should rely on other sources for specific information like this. Older people's memories of childhood tend to be surprisingly good and wartime experiences also tend to remain very vivid with people simply because they were living under extraordinary circumstances. Many people will also remember special occasions, such as the day they saw their first aeroplane fly over or the day the king visited the town.

Sometimes you may find it helpful to take along memory joggers such as old photographs or postcards which will often spark off a train of memories. Any prompt which appeals to the senses can potentially be of use – playing a popular old folk song on tape, for instance. You could also try asking your interviewees if they have any photos or mementoes from the time you are asking about, as this will serve both as a memory prompt for them and could provide more material for you. Many people have interesting pieces of memorabilia about the home which you may want to draw attention to at an appropriate moment, if your interviewees have not done so already. Getting several people together of roughly the same age is also a good way of getting the memories flowing. With particularly elderly or frail people, be aware of how much time you are spending with them – reminiscing can be quite tiring even if most people enjoy it. If you envisage doing a lot of work with elderly people a useful book is *Reminiscence Work with Old People* by Clare Gillies and Anne James (see *Booklist*). Although this is aimed primarily at social and health care professionals it provides valuable guidance on communicating with elderly people and ways of getting the memories flowing.

Interviewing the rich and famous

If your interviewee is a celebrity or earns more in five minutes than you will earn in a year, you may well feel a little overwhelmed. Whilst this is understandable, you need to remember that you are meeting them on equal terms as a professional, not as an adoring fan. Very successful people have usually become so because they are both disciplined and professional – prima donnas are more likely to be amongst the ranks of the also rans. People who are in the public eye usually have both an image and a reputation to live up to and your write-up is therefore important to them. Don't forget that behind the hype, facade or gold bath taps they are still members of the human race. The rich and famous are like everybody else underneath and a good interviewer should be talking to the part of them that eats, sleeps and breathes. If you find someone very intimidating you could always try to imagine him picking his nose.

Interviewing politicians

This is not the easy way to start an interviewing career. Politicians are specially trained to fend off awkward questions and to prevaricate. Don't expect to get a straight answer if some of the biggest journalists on television can't. If you have to interview a politician, it might be best to start with your local politician and ask them about their garden – you may or may not get a straight answer.

Interviewing and anonymity

In some interviews you may have to deal with interviewees who do not want to be identified with the piece you are writing but are none the less willing to talk to you. There are many reasons why a person may not want to be directly identified with an interview – people who are involved in criminal activity, prostitution or who are talking about difficult personal experiences may not like to have their names displayed before thousands. If you anticipate that you may encounter this kind of difficulty, you could offer to preserve a person's anonymity when you are arranging the interview. If you feel that someone is wavering about giving you an interview for reasons like this, offer to let them be interviewed under a pseudonym and say that you will not write about them in a way which would make them recognizable, e.g. by giving very precise details as to their appearance and where they live or work. Sometimes you may feel it is appropriate to offer the subjects the choice of anonymity whether they have raised the issue or not, or at least to check with them during the interview that they do not mind being identified. Some people may not realize the full implications of being exposed to thousands of readers and the potential effect this may have on them. For more on this see under chapter 11, *Transcribing and writing up.*

They want to see the questions first

Occasionally your interviewees may request a copy of your questions before the interview. There may be several reasons for this for instance:

- Your interviewees are very busy and need to know exactly what is expected of them at a particular time.
- Your interviewees need briefing (this is often the case with politicians who have to appear informed on a large number of topics with which they may not be directly familiar).
- Their first language may not be English so they may need more time to prepare their answers.
- They may be paranoid (perhaps with good reason) that you are about to do a nasty investigative piece on them.
- They may be worried about 'getting it wrong'.
- They may have a very understandable fear of the unknown.

Whilst some of these reasons may be perfectly valid (the first three for example) you may feel that the request for questions is generated more by anxiety than from a genuine need to see the questions beforehand. Whether you decide to submit questions is down to your discretion but as a very general rule it is not really a good idea to let your interviewee see what you want to ask first – you will tend to get rather flat, formulated answers. For journalists in particular this can be difficult if you are hoping to get some lively interesting copy for your piece (although very occasionally it might work to your advantage with the interviewee who has spent sleepless nights trying to think of the wittiest answers possible). Another drawback for the interviewer is that you may feel more inhibited about what you can ask if you have to submit questions first and you may find yourself sticking to very safe (and perhaps not terribly interesting) questions.

If you are asked to submit questions you could try saying something like 'It's not really editorial policy to show someone the questions first', or 'I'm not sure exactly which questions I am going to ask you yet but they will be quite general and straightforward and there's really nothing to worry about.' If your subjects insist on seeing the questions first, you can either let them see them or lose the interview. All is not lost if you do decide to send a list of questions – you will almost certainly still get something worthwhile from the interview and, even though you may have submitted a set list of questions, there is nothing to stop you slipping in further questions, once the interview is under way. There is no guarantee, of course, that your interviewees will answer them but at this point in the interview you will have had time to build up a rapport with them so they may be willing to answer extra questions anyway.

Forbidden questions

Sometimes your interviewee, prior to doing the interview, may make it a condition that you do not ask questions about certain things such as the recent break-up of a marriage. This will tend to happen more with celebrity interviews. If your sole interest in the interviewees is to find out about their private life you have the following options:
- Give up and find someone else to interview.
- Secure the interview and slip your questions in through the back door when the interview is well under way. This is not something to attempt at your first interview and, if you decide to adopt this approach, you should also be prepared for the fact that you might be shown the back door yourself.
- Try talking them in to it. Say why it's important that they talk about the recent break-up of their marriage – offer to set the record straight, let them know that you are sympathetic to their position.

If someone has already agreed to give you an interview but tells you when you turn up or when you first raise a related question that that subject is taboo, you can adopt a softly softly approach whereby you establish a rapport with your interviewee and then try asking when the interview is well under way. It is best not to do it in an underhand way – try something like: 'I know you said you didn't want to talk about your divorce when we first started but I wondered whether it might be helpful just to set the record straight for the public to avoid all the rumour and speculation that's been flying around. . .'

Off the record

If people have agreed to be interviewed, they are automatically agreeing to let you write up what they say during the interview. However, at some point in the interview your interviewees may say something that they had not intended to say or realise that what they say may be quite damaging ('Of course, my ex-wife was a cow from day one.'). They may retract by adding 'That's off the record'. You are honourably bound to comply with someone saying 'off the record' even if it means losing the best quote of the day. You can occasionally bypass this if you can get a quote from someone else quoting what your interviewee said ('He told me he always thought his wife was a cow,') but be wary of getting into unintentional libel (see under *Transcribing and writing up*). Sometimes you might want to censor what is said yourself, if you feel people may have unwittingly incriminated themselves or you may at least want to ask something like: 'Are you sure you don't mind me saying that you used to shop-lift out of Marks and Spencers when you didn't have any money?'

They want to see what you've written

It is not uncommon for interviewees to ask to look at your piece before it goes to press or to the editor. In many ways this is understandable – allowing yourself to be interviewed for a publication can seem a risky business and interviewees may well want to have some control over what does and does not get said about them in public. There are occasions when showing your article to the interviewee should be avoided at all costs and occasions when it's probably a very good idea.

When not to show it to your interviewee

When I was quite new to interviewing a very pleasant interviewee asked if he could see the article I was writing about him before I sent it off to the intended magazine. I agreed rather reluctantly, although I had heard that it was probably not good policy. I soon found out why as a general rule interviewees should not see the piece that is written about them. The first difficulty was timing. I had a deadline for the piece that was quite close – two weeks away. By the time I had posted my piece off and received a reply eight days had passed. It was getting too close to the deadline for comfort. The second difficulty was that my interviewee had decided that he did not like the way I had written up one or two quotes – whilst I had recorded them accurately, he had decided that something would sound better with a word in a different position. The interviewee also decided that he wanted to expand on something he had told me and was oblivious to the fact that, although I had a 1000-word limit, he was expecting me to incorporate another 100 words. Finally, he had made a number of minor corrections which he thought improved the piece. Whilst he did not attempt to make any major changes and had generally liked the piece I found myself faced with what I felt were a number of unnecessary corrections with my deadline only a few days off. In the end I did not make the corrections (I had not given any undertaking that I would) but I had wasted a lot of precious time by letting my interviewee see it. In this case it was completely unnecessary to let the interviewee see the finished product and the situation could have been made worse if he had decided that a number of major changes were required. This example highlights four main reasons why it is not usually a good idea to show someone what you have written about them:

- It will hold you up in submitting your work and possibly missing your deadline which will not endear you to the editor.
- Interviewees will always want to change it, no matter what you write or how you write it.
- Even if you quote them accurately, they may decide that they wish they had either said it differently or said something else.
- They may want to add to or subtract from what you have already written. If you are working to a tight word limit this may not be feasible.

The general rule is that, unless there is a very good reason for showing someone your finished product (see below), do not show it to them. Your interviewees have agreed to let you interview them and vetting your piece is not part of the agreement. How you choose to write up the piece is your concern. It is probably inevitable that they will pick up on something that they felt could have been done differently when they see your article but remember you are the writer, not them.

If someone asks to see what you have written try to refuse tactfully. You can simply say outright 'I'm sorry it's not editorial policy to do that,' although I often prefer to say 'It's not the usual policy but I could mention to the editor that you'd like to see it. . .' In this way I take the onus off myself and pass it to the editor without making any commitment. Most people find editors a rather terrifying species and so no more will be said about it. You could also reassure them at this point that you are not going to write anything libellous or false. If your interviewees have made it a condition of doing the interview that you show them the finished product before sending it off for publication, you are honour bound at least to show them. Alternatively find different interviewees.

When to show it to your interviewee

There are occasions when it is in everyone's best interests (you, the interviewee, the publication and the reader) to have the piece checked over before you submit it. It is usually a very good idea to show your finished piece to an expert whom you have interviewed. In particular if you are dealing with matters which you know little about (the growth of the ball-bearing industry in Sweden, for instance) and are not 100 per cent sure that you have got all your facts right, getting an expert to cast his eye over what you have written is a very sensible thing to do. Whilst, in the case of the ball-bearing industry, getting a few minor facts wrong might cause some irritation, there are occasions when getting the facts wrong can cause serious problems both for you and the publication.

If you are writing a medical piece for instance, giving the wrong advice could have serious consequences, not only for someone who follows the wrong advice, but for the doctor or medical expert whom you consulted for the article. The doctor's reputation is at stake here and you as the interviewer have at least a moral duty not to jeopardise it – in an extreme case you may have a libel suit on your hands. I was once nearly refused an interview with a consultant gynaecologist on the grounds that she was no longer giving press interviews because what she said had been misrepresented in a popular women's magazine. The gynaecologist had an additional grievance – the journalist who had interviewed her previously had promised to let her see the article before it went for publication but had not honoured this agreement. In the end the doctor agreed to talk to me (probably because I had listened sympathetically to her grievances and offered not to use her name directly in the piece), but her grievances were perfectly understandable. She should have been sent the article before it was sent for publication.

The main reasons for letting your interviewees see your piece are:
• To check technical and specialist knowledge.
• To ensure overall accuracy.
• To make sure that their reputation has not been compromised.

- So that you can assure editors, when you submit it, that the work has been checked.

See also under chapter 12, *Afterwards*, for more on forwarding copy for the interviewee to check.

Meeting in a pub or restaurant

Occasionally your prospective interviewee may suggest that you meet in a pub or restaurant. This is fine if it suits both of you but you should bear in mind the following points before agreeing to it.

Who pays the bill?

Journalists in particular have a tradition of exchanging a meal or a pint in return for an interview or for the information given. Whilst staff journalists can often draw on company expenses to fund restaurant bills, if you are a freelance writer you should consider carefully whether you can really afford to stand someone a meal. You need to weigh up how much it is likely to eat into the profits you are expecting to make from your writing before you agree to meet over a meal. Most interviewees will not expect anything in exchange but some will, so bear this in mind before you agree to meet someone at lunchtime at the Ritz. A way round this is to agree to meet at a time other than lunch or dinner time and preferably not at the Ritz. Buying someone a cup of tea or coffee or a pint is reasonable, given the help they are giving you and you should expect to pick up the bill for small items.

The noise factor

Some eating and drinking places can be quite noisy so if you are using a tape recorder you may find that there is a lot of background noise or even that you are actually unable to hear what the person is saying. If this is the case, have a secondary plan to move on to somewhere quieter.

Eat first, talk later

If you are having a meal you will probably find that it is not easy to devote whole-hearted attention to your interviewee and to wrap tagliatelle round your fork at the same time and it is almost impossible to take notes whilst breaking into a pavlova. Make small talk over the meal and get down to the serious business of interviewing after the serious business of eating.

They want to meet you afterwards

You may find that you get on particularly well with some individuals you are interviewing. They may ask you if you would like to meet them afterwards. It's up to you whether you decide you want to see them or not but do be wary about letting any socializing come between you and your piece. Your loyalty is to your writing and to your editor first and you should not allow yourself to become compromised. Chatting over a drink after the interview can be very pleasant and is one of the bonuses of a good interview.

You want another go

If an interview goes well but you find that you have not really had time to cover everything you need to cover or can see that there is even more interesting material to be unearthed, rather than extending the interview time there and then it is often more appropriate to ask if you can have a second interview. Writers or researchers who are dealing with a subject in depth may need to do this as a matter of course. If you have only arranged to do one interview but feel that you need more time ask your interviewee if you can meet again. Saying something like 'This is really useful material but I don't think I'm going to be able to do justice to what you are saying after just one interview – would it be possible to meet again at a convenient time?' will probably persuade them if they need any persuading.

Long interviews

In some ways having a second go is better than making the first interview very long. When you are interviewing you should bear in mind both the tiredness and boredom factor. If you are interviewing well, you are giving your interviewee 100 per cent attention which can become mentally draining when sustained for any length of time. For the persons being interviewed, especially if they are not used to it, the drain can be even greater, although often nervous energy will carry them through. Biographers and people who may be doing extensive interviews with one particular person will need to make a break. Whilst some people can carry on talking all afternoon, you will probably find that two hours is enough for most people. Obviously if you have just uncovered the story of the century or you feel that it would be difficult for the interviewees to take up where they left off again, see it through as far as you can. Whilst most people like to be interviewed when they have got over their initial nervousness, it's up to the interviewer to remember not to inconvenience the interviewees too much as they may well be very busy. On the whole it's not a good idea to interview for so long that it is the interviewee who finishes the interview, not you, although this may not always be avoidable.

10
TROUBLE-SHOOTING

You will probably find that you can negotiate most interviews without encountering too many difficulties but interviews are no exception to Murphy's Law and inevitably something may go wrong. What follows is a brief overview of some of the more common problems that might arise in interviewing and how to deal with them. Perhaps the most important point to remember is that, if you are unfortunate enough to have a bad interview, it is not the end of the world and there are many more good interviews out there waiting for you. If you have a bad interview or if something goes unexpectedly wrong, put it down to experience, see what you can learn from it and move on to the next one.

Hostile interviewees

There may be several reasons why interviewees are hostile. They may just be nervous and therefore defensive, be having a particularly bad day or simply be an unpleasant character. They may have had a bad experience with interviewers previously or they may only be granting an interview because it's part of their job description (press officers, for example) or because their agent has arranged it for them. You may be the sixth person they've seen that day and perhaps there are other things they would rather be doing with their time. Some interviewees may enjoy having a power hold over you and want you to grovel at their feet before they part with their precious information or maybe they are just looking for someone to avenge themselves on for a previous bad experience.

There are numerous possibilities but the question that you will probably be asking yourself is 'Is it me?' I have only experienced one hostile interviewee but the outcome shows that an unpleasant interview may have nothing to do with you at all. I was interviewing the personnel manager of one of the country's most prestigious hotels for an article for a local interest magazine. I felt from the start that she did not want to do the interview, although she had seemed willing enough over the phone; she never so much as smiled as I walked in the door, spoke in a condescending patronising way which occasionally betrayed outright impatience and ordered coffee for herself without offering me any. My first assumption was that I was doing something wrong but I couldn't understand exactly what it was. I managed to hold the interview together by focusing on my questions and adopting an efficient, professional stance which saw me through but I came away with a very unpleasant feeling.

About a year later I read in the paper that the same person was appealing against dismissal from her post. I later learned from a contact that she had been dismissed for treating people in the way she had treated me. The moral of the story is that you should not automatically assume that the fault lies with you. This happened fairly early on a career as a freelance journalist and, had I not had some excellent subjects for interview prior to this, I might have had second thoughts about wanting to do any more. Don't allow a bad interview to deprive you of all the pleasure of the good ones yet to come.

Whilst you need to be aware that you might be the sole cause of the hostility (maybe you are being over familiar, too cold, staring too much, etc.) and may need to make certain adjustments in what you are doing, don't automatically assume that you personally are the cause of it. True, your interviewees may sometimes actively dislike what they think you represent (journalists, in particular, sometimes come up against this kind of prejudice when they are all lumped together in someone's mind as the nastier breed of tabloid hack), but there is a clear distinction between what you are doing and who you are.

Whether you feel that the person is objecting to your role or to you personally the most important thing is to try not to let it affect your carrying out your interview. This is where professionalism counts. There is no contract that states that the interviewees should like you (although you will probably get a better interview if they do). So long as you can communicate effectively together, personalities needn't come into it at all. Of course, it is much more pleasant for everyone concerned if the interview goes well and you end up liking each other, but it's certainly not a failure if you don't.

Revenge or not?

The advice sometimes given to trainee journalists is 'Get your revenge on paper, not in person.' Whether you want to follow this advice is a matter for your own discretion but it is certainly not a good idea to retaliate there and then because you risk losing the interview altogether. No matter what you are feeling, remain detached and professional. Revenge on paper does not necessarily mean writing a wholly negative and possibly libellous account but, if the tone of the interview has significantly coloured your view, you may be able to incorporate it to your advantage into your writing. If your interviewee was really awful, simply reproducing parts of the interview verbatim without expressing any personal opinions is often all you need to do. Be very wary of trying to put someone down in an article – what passes for cleverness may be mere cattiness. If you can do it well, fine. If not leave well alone – you may have a libel suit on your hands amongst other things. In the final analysis you should remember that at the very least you are going to be paid for putting up with the hostility and you always have the option of walking out.

Make it work for you

In some kinds of writing you have quite a bit of discretion about how you write up an interview and you can actually make an unpleasant interview into a triumph. A profile feature in one of the Sunday papers offers a case in point of how this can be done. The interviewer had interviewed a male actor who was obviously hostile to her from the minute she walked in the door. He used every opportunity to put her and what she was doing down. The interviewer wrote up the interview as if it were a fight in a boxing ring with ten rounds in which she systematically recorded his hostility and aggression until the final knock-out. It was very funny to read and, whilst it probably wasn't much fun for the interviewer at the time, she had turned something potentially degrading and nasty into a triumph.

You don't like them

You may at some point find yourself interviewing people whom you dislike either for personal reasons or for the views they express and sometimes both. In fact, it is quite possible that you could specifically want to interview someone whose opinions you strongly disagree with – a member of the Nazi party, for instance, or a member of a paedophile ring. If this is the case you should keep your personal opinions to yourself as you are not doing the interview to have an argument. You can, of course, query what is being said by playing devil's advocate, e.g. 'Some people might say that boxing is simply organised violence. How would you respond to that view?' but do not present opinions as if they were your own (for more on expressing personal opinions see chapter 8, *Conducting the interview*). At best you will alienate your interviewees, at worst they may throw you out.

If you do not like the person, be aware of how your own personal prejudices may be affecting your view. It is not a sin or a crime to be young/old, male/female, white/black/mixed race, intelligent/low IQ, rich/poor, live in a caravan/live in a manor house, etc., etc. As well as affecting the interview, unconscious prejudices can also inadvertently affect your writing. Try to be honest about it and put your prejudices to one side for at least the duration of the interview. The interviewees are doing you a favour in seeing you in the first place and as a guest on both their time and possibly their territory, you should always treat them with respect.

If you do not like people because of the way they behave or seem to be in themselves, you may need to make allowances for interview nerves. Interviews can do strange things to people – not least imbue them with an inflated sense of their own importance (this is as true for someone being interviewed about their prize marrows for the local parish magazine as it is for an up-and-coming star in one of the magazine glossies). The same can also be said for some interviewers. Don't assume you are on a higher plane just because you are holding the tape recorder.

If you find you are still unable to like them remember that, as with their liking you, there is nothing in the agreement about liking or otherwise – just treat them with respect and remain professional and detached.

You like them too much

A problem sometimes encountered by interviewers is that they end up liking their subject so much that this, rather than the needs of the publication, colour the way it is written. People who interview over a long period of time can be particularly prone to this. They may come to know and like their interviewee very much and may feel that they do not want to write anything that is less than complimentary. Whilst there is nothing intrinsically wrong with liking your interviewee above and beyond the call of your project, you always need to bear in mind that your loyalty is to the publication. If you are aware of this before you start out it is less likely to become a problem.

It may be dangerous

Interviewing can take you into all sorts of weird and wonderful places and some of them may be less salubrious than others. If your writing or research leads you into a potentially dangerous situation (for example, interviewing street prostitutes in an area known for violence), tell someone where you are going beforehand and when they should expect you back. If possible ask a friend to wait round the corner for you. Sometimes it might be feasible to do this kind of interview with someone else – two female staff journalists might go together for instance – but, if you are on your own as a freelance, take as many precautions as you can. Don't put your writing above your personal safety – you're probably not being paid enough.

The Interviewee is drunk/incapacitated

Interviewing someone who is somewhat under the influence is not necessarily a disaster. Some people become more fluent and can be quite amusing when their inhibitions are down. It is all a question of degree. In some circles being partly sozzled is part of a day's routine, particularly if liquid lunches are involved. But if someone is so drunk or spaced out by drugs that the interview doesn't make sense, it is better to halt it and ask if you can come at another time. There is little point in becoming irritated – irritation is usually lost on drunk people anyway, but be firm and polite and try to smile about it. After all, to some people it may be a great joke.

Uses of restraint

Sometimes when an interview is well under way, your interviewees may let something slip or do something that they would probably rather was not recorded in print. If they say afterwards that it is off the record, they have covered themselves but, if they do not and you feel that they have said something which may be either damaging to themselves or someone else, you may need to query it. If they have said something that is a potential scoop ('Clean-living Christian Megastar says drugs should be legalised'), you may be torn between scooping and pooping. Check with them: 'Is that on or off the record?' or 'That's really interesting – is it all right if I use that in my piece?' This way you have covered your own back if you get their consent on tape. If they say something that could potentially damage another party, don't use it. This is getting into the area of libel (see chapter 11, *Transcribing and writing up* for more on libel).

You are bored

Unfortunately all interviewing isn't about going out and talking to your favourite authors about their best book. It could happen that you get interviewees who seem to send you to sleep as soon as they open their mouth. Possibly the subject matter is less than riveting and you really aren't that interested in the gas industry's corporate sales to Outer Mongolia. No matter how much you may occasionally find some people or the subject matter boring, don't ever let them feel that this is what you are thinking. Apart from its being bad manners, you are going to get an even worse response if they feel that they are boring you. Focus on the job you are doing. Very often simply wanting to get the information (whatever it is) can override your lack of interest in the contents and, if you are writing for a publication your readers may be fascinated by the subject, even if you are not.

They seem bored

Perhaps they are. Perhaps they've done three interviews already this morning and perhaps every interviewer has asked the same questions. You could try asking a surprising question to jolt them out of their inertia like 'What do you hate most about interviews?' but don't worry too much about it – there is nothing down in writing to say that they should be interested, and so long as you get the information you came for it doesn't matter how bored they are. Sometimes what you perceive as boredom may just be a cover for anxiety. If you really can't engage their interest in you or your questions, just focus on getting the answers. Bored interviewees are fairly rare – you are far more likely to find that the interviewee is overawed.

Over-anxious interviewees

If people are over-anxious they will find it difficult to focus on the question you are asking. They may go off at an odd tangent, what they say may become confused or they may find it very hard to say anything at all. Usually their body language will also give you an indication that they are anxious – they may be breathing too quickly, sitting too rigidly, staring at you or not making any eye contact at all. The important point is that you do not allow their anxiety to affect you. Stay in control and stay calm – they will pick this up off you. Take it slowly and, if they go off the subject or don't make a lot of sense gently bring them back by saying something like 'Can I just go over this again because it's really useful and I want to get it right. . .' In this way you are being quite flattering by letting them know that what they are saying is useful (flattery can be a very useful tool for interviewees so long as it doesn't come across as insincerity) and you are also putting yourself in a human light by letting them know that you can make mistakes and are concerned to get it right. If they are silent or answering in monosyllables, and you think this is due to anxiety, you will have to do a certain amount of thinking on your feet. If the questions are correctly phrased they should not invite a monosyllabic answer (see chapter 6, under *Framing the question*), but, if you are getting very short answers which are not really telling you very much, try drawing the answers out a little by asking more questions. Keep your questions simple, smile and nod at the answers to give encouragement.

If the interview really does grind to a halt and you feel that your interviewee cannot continue, suggest that you have a short break from the questions – if it seems appropriate ask 'Shall we have a cup of tea now?' Try to take the focus away from the interview by talking about something else – the cat or the pictures on the wall, for instance. Very often simply encouraging someone to talk about anything will get the ball rolling. You may want to raise the interviewees' difficulties in an indirect way by saying something like: 'It must be really hard work being interviewed – I always wonder how I'd be able to cope with it if it was me being interviewed', or you may want to reassure them that it doesn't matter that they are not getting it perfect first time (anxious interviewees are often over concerned with getting it right), e.g. 'What you're telling me is really useful – I'll sort out the bits I don't want later when I come to transcribe the tape.' See also under *Explaining the process* in chapter 8, *Conducting the interview.*

The interview is unusable

Sometimes you may go to an interview and realise before you are very far into it that the interviewees have nothing to contribute to what you are writing. They may not have the information you need or what they say might be unusable for a number of reasons (it is libellous, irrelevant, a personal ego trip, etc.). In this case you have to decide whether it is better to simply cut the interview short or to continue without any intention of using it. On the whole it is more tactful to continue (no one likes to be told that what they are saying is useless, no matter how delicately it is put), unless the information is purely factual and the interviewees have no personal vested interest in what they are saying. If you do cut the interview short (this is most easily done in a telephone interview), thank them for their help and say something like 'I think I really need to speak to someone who is familiar with. . . for this one.' If you decide to continue, keep it as short as possible and thank them for their help at the end (even if they haven't really given you any). If the interview was wholly unusable (and it very rarely is), you will need to find other subjects to interview.

Another reason why you may not be able to make use of the interview is that you may interview several other people who give you better information or because you simply have too much material to be able to use all of it. A difficulty which you may subsequently encounter is that your interviewees are eagerly waiting to see their name and what they have said in print and are highly disappointed when nothing comes of it. If you are writing a book, you can usually compensate them by acknowledging their 'help' at the front (see chapter 12, under *Acknowledgements*) but, if it is a piece for a magazine or newspaper and your interviewees ring you up, demanding to know where their name got to in the piece, you may just have to say that, whilst they were very helpful, constraints of space made it impossible to include what they have said in the article. You could always let them know that you are not going to use what they have said, but you are under no obligation to (there has been no agreement to this effect); additionally it is only a possibility that they will contact you when the piece has been published so you could just be creating an unnecessary problem for yourself. Unfortunately not being able to use all the material is fairly common and, whilst this is a great disappointment to the interviewee, there is little that you can do about it as your loyalty ultimately is to your writing or research.

Explaining it to the editor

If you have gone to an interview and found it completely unusable and are unable to complete your piece because the interview was essential, you will need to explain this to the intended editor if you have been given a commission or at least a sign of interest. Editors should understand and, if the fact that the interview was unusable is not your fault, they should be willing to look at further work from you. You can always offer a similar alternative piece if you can think of one.

They aren't there

This can be very annoying, especially if you have made elaborate travel arrangements to arrive on time. If they are not in when you call, it is usually because they have either forgotten the appointment or something else more pressing has turned up. Give them time (how much is up to you). If there is a secretary, leave a message letting your prospective interviewee know that you called. When you find a convenient moment ring your lost interviewee and ask what has happened. No matter how irritating and inconvenient it has been for you, try not to get annoyed with him or her in person as you may be able to retrieve the situation by arranging the interview for another time. Usually if people have let you down, they will feel guilty and be eager to make good the mistake.

You miss the appointment

If you miss the appointment – either because your best-laid plans went astray or you simply forgot – you can try to retrieve the situation by ringing your interviewee as soon as possible. If you have a valid reason (such as your car breaking down on the way or a bomb scare at the train station), you will find most people sympathetic, although there is of course no guarantee that they will be able to offer you another interview. If you simply forgot or over-slept, it is probably not a good idea to ring up and say so – it would sound as if you do not care and were unprofessional in your approach. A few choice white lies might be the better option. If you discover on the way there that you are not going to make it or are going to be late, it is a matter of courtesy to let your interviewee know. If you are going to be late, you can allay a lot of your own anxiety by ringing up beforehand or on the way. By following the advice outlined in chapter 6, you should be prepared for this. If you happen to break down in the middle of a prairie where phone boxes are thin on the ground, there is probably nothing you can do except accept the situation philosophically.

Perks versus bribes

Being a writer can bring many unexpected pleasures. Whilst these are rarely financial ones, it is not unusual, in particular for journalists, to receive free gifts or free trials in the process of researching and interviewing. This can range from the original free lunch to a paid holiday with many variations in between. Very often these perks are given partly to help the writer in the process of researching (it would be difficult to write about the latest malt whisky without ever having allowed it to trickle over your palate), although the tacit reason might be the hope of influencing the writer to write something favourable about a product, a person, a place or an experience (there really is no such thing as a free lunch). There is nothing wrong with this, providing the agreement is tacit and writers are not compromising the integrity of what they are writing for the sake of a free gift. If in the course of interviewing you encounter unexpected spin-offs like an invitation to spend a weekend in an historic home, for instance, accept them graciously and enjoy them, but don't allow yourself to become compromised. Your duty is to your publication, not to the person who is making life pleasant for you. Do not feel under any obligation to go along with people who are offering you something on the condition that you write something good about it – they do not have the right to ask this of you, although with friends this is rather more difficult to refuse. If you feel yourself being put in this position, be polite but non-committal ('I'll certainly look forward to sampling this champagne at the weekend'). You probably will enjoy it but you are under no obligation to your interviewee to say that you have enjoyed it in print.

They want money

If your interviewee wants to be paid, you should tell them outright that you never pay. Good interviewees cannot be bought and, whilst the interview may be of benefit to you, it will very often be the case that your interviewees are benefiting from it in some way too, either from publicity or prestige. If they insist, you could say that it is not editorial policy. There may be times when certain people are so essential to your work that you cannot possibly write it without their help, and you may be willing to pay up, but these cases are exceptions and as a general rule you should hang on to your cheque book. Cheque-book journalism may work for established writers for the tabloids but this money is coming out of newspaper expenses, and unless this is the direction you hope your writing career will follow, do not pay for any interview.

This does not preclude you from picking up the bill in a cafe, restaurant or pub, or from offering to pay travel expenses if someone comes to meet you.

You don't get the answers you expected

If you go to an interview with too fixed an idea in your head as to what the answers should be, you are liable to be disappointed. In fact it raises the question as to why, if you know all the answers, you want to ask the questions in the first place. The problem here is having too fixed an idea before you start. If, for example, you plan an article about 'How Mr Bloggs enjoys his retirement' and you find out that actually Mr Bloggs absolutely hates his retirement and wants to be back at work, you will have to change your whole conception of what the article is going to be about. Similarly the biographical subject you thought you were going to love may turn out to be the most ghastly human being that ever walked the earth. For these kinds of reasons articles and pieces of research should be exploratory. You might start off with a hypothesis but it is intrinsic to the nature of any research that you may be forced to alter your ideas in the process of carrying it out and interviewing is no exception to this. Sometimes your hypothesis may be totally disproved but this is by no means a disaster – research can often be turned on its head. One false trail can lead to a new fresh one.

You forget the questions

If you have followed the precautions outlined in chapter 6, this should not happen. Until you are completely confident about your ability to put questions off the top of your head to anyone you meet, never leave home without your question prompts. Always keep your notebook with your questions within seeing distance at the interview. If you do forget and have no source of prompts to hand, it can be embarrassing to the point of devastating. At best it is an experience which you are never likely to repeat. The only way you can retrieve this situation is to think on your feet about the kinds of questions you need to ask or to ask your interviewee if you can do it on another day.

Failed tape recorder

Again, if you have taken suitable precautions (see chapter 6) this should not happen but technology is not always bound by 'shoulds' and 'oughts' and, if you find that your tape recorder has not picked up the interview or if you drop it in a puddle on the way home, you have the following options:

- If you can remember the important things that were said and your piece is not heavily dependent on the quotes you gleaned from the interviewee, you should be able to manage on memory providing that you write it down straight away. You should also be able to check any uncertainties by ringing up your interviewee.
- If you are unable to remember the contents of the interview or feel that you have missed out on some necessary quotes, you can always try ringing your interviewee and asking if you can have another go. In practice you will probably not need to repeat the whole interview and may be able to get what you need over the phone.

- You can guard against this ever happening by combining note-taking with recording. Some interviewers even take two tape recorders along to each session.

Failed camera

In the first interview I ever did, I thought I had done everything right until I got home to discover that my camera had not had any film in it. Whilst this sounds like a very stupid mistake (and in fact it was), it had happened because I had automatically assumed that there was a film in the camera. I had not used the camera for some time and I had been too busy worrying about where to go, getting there on time and how my interviewee would react to a novice like myself to check the real basics. As the magazine I was writing for insisted on a photograph, I had no choice but to ring up my interviewee and ask if I could come and take another one (I invented a story about how someone had opened the camera by mistake and the film was ruined). This was not a problem and in fact I gained some more valuable quotes and insights at my second attempt, but it was a mistake that I would hate to make again. If your camera fails you or the film is ruined and you are expected to provide a photograph, your only real option is to ring up and ask to do it again or to ask them to provide a photograph, of themselves. If someone has an agent, that is a possible source of a photo. Probably the only real insurance against a failed camera is to take two cameras which will also allow you to take a black and white and a colour photo.

11
TRANSCRIBING AND WRITING UP

This is the point at which you remember that interviewing is only a part of the writing and researching process and not an end in itself. Even though you may feel that you have already done rather a lot of work for your piece, there is still a long way to go before the interview is successfully transferred on to your word-processor or finds approval on an editor's desk. In this chapter we will look at ways of ordering and preparing your work to a professional standard.

So, with the most difficult part over with you now come to one of the less stimulating parts of interviewing – transcribing the tape.

Transcribing

If you have recorded your interview you are now going to have to put it into a readable format. To do this you will need to transcribe the tape contents by writing down what was said. Although this may at first seem time consuming (and even worse you will have to sit through listening to your-self on tape), transcribing the tape contents will pay dividends in terms of helping you to clarify the material you have and in deciding which parts you want to use in your writing. The golden rule of transcribing is do it as soon as possible – preferably on the same day. There are several reasons for this but some of the main ones are:

- The interview is fresh in your mind and you can put in your own responses to what was said and how the interviewee was looking and behaving at the time. See under adding *Your own information* below.
- You are able to see whether anything significant is missing or needs checking. You can then follow this up straight away instead of letting time elapse until both you and your interviewee have only a hazy recall of the interview.
- The sooner you transcribe the interview the sooner you can get on with writing it up.

It is not necessary to write down everything on the tape because some of it will patently not be of any use to you – lengthy digressions being a case in point – and nor is it usually necessary to write down the questions again. If you are writing a piece with a particular angle, it should become immediately apparent which parts are going to be particularly useful: if you are writing a largely factual piece you will obviously be homing in on the straight, factual information given to you by your interviewee with appro-priate quotes; if you are doing a profile you will be particularly interested in anything that is revealing about the person and any 'quotable quotes' which may be surprising, funny or which add meat to your interview; if you are writing about local history you will be particularly interested in any details or information about the locality. Freelance journalists hoping to sell a number of articles from the same interview will probably want to take down as much as possible from the tape to see which parts can be used for different articles (see also chapter 12).

Transcribing a tape's contents can be quite time consuming but unless you have access to a secretary there are no real shortcuts. If you have a word-processor with a 'cut and paste' facility (i.e. you can move blocks of texts around), you will be able to save time by writing the transcription directly on to the computer and then moving relevant blocks of text to fit into your writing. Otherwise you will need to type the transcription or write it in longhand. This is where a pedal-operated tape recorder comes into its own. For an hour's interview you may need to set aside two or three hours and sometimes longer to get down everything you need. At the transcribing stage you do not need to concern yourself too much with how something is said as you will deal with this at the writing-up stage. For the moment just concentrate on writing the tape contents.

When transcribing the tape it helps to do the following:

- Listen to it all the way through making a note of the exact position of particularly useful information by writing down the tape counter number.
- Play the tape again, fast forwarding to the position where the quote or information you need is. Write down what you need (you will probably need to replay it several times over the same part to make sure that you have the words accurately).
- Listen to the tape again when you have finished so that you are satisfied that you have got everything you need.
- When you have got everything you need, store the tape in a safe place. Do not throw it away or record over it. See under *libel* below for more about storing tapes. Keep your transcription in a safe place too.

Adding your own information

As you are transcribing the tape you may want to add brief notes of your own in addition to those you may have made at the interview. If the interviewees have said something like 'I'm at the age where I need to take stock of my life and try to make some sense of it all', you may recall what they were looking like when they said it – were they looking sad, peaceful, worried? Did their body language change – did they look wistfully out of the window, raise their eyes to heaven, cross themselves or take a gulp of beer? What kind of tone did they use, what nuances can you pick up from the tape and what do you remember yourself from the way it sounded? If you are transcribing the interview straight away, these details should still be with you. Put them in next to the quote you have transcribed as a memory prompt to yourself for when you are ready to write up. This need be only a simple one-word trigger such as 'crossed' for crossed himself. If you put it in square brackets '[crossed]', you will know that it is your addition not something that the interviewee said. When you come to write up your final piece you may want to include this kind of detail. Obviously these kinds of details will only be appropriate for certain kinds of writing. No one will really want to know that the scientist you interviewed for a technical magazine about the latest discovery in washing powder is looking tired and in need of a holiday nor would it be appropriate to start making puns about how washed out he looked.

Making sense of notes

If you have opted to write notes instead of recording, you will not need to go through the transcription process but you will probably want to add to what you have written and you may want to impose your own order on the notes (see below under *Ordering the transcription*). It is unlikely that you will have managed to get down everything your interviewee said but, if you have used a private note taking system or used prompt words for the bits you did not get, you can add what you accurately remember after the interview. Because of the accuracy problem it is very important that you make any additional notes as soon as possible.

Checking it

If you suspect that something that your interviewee has told you may be wrong, always check it. Experts are human too – they can forget or get the facts mixed up just like the rest of us. You can check it with them by making a quick phone call and saying something like 'I didn't manage to pick up what you said about the number of times you were shot down in World War Two. Could you just remind me?' Do not supply a tentative answer yourself, e.g. 'Was it three times you were shot down or thirteen?', as this may influence the answer. You can try to verify non-personal facts through written sources.

Ordering the transcription

When you have transcribed the tape you will probably find that you have a daunting amount of writing in front of you – probably far more than you can use for your writing. You will also almost certainly find that your transcription has no particular order to it, that your interviewee has inconveniently ranged from subject to subject and back again with other bits thrown in at peculiar junctions. The next step is to impose some order on the jumble of information in front of you. It is often helpful to group your information according to themes or subjects – for instance, bringing together all the information on childhood and family background and then all the material on career success, etc. There are various methods you can use to do this. Probably the simplest is to use highlighter pens of a variety of colours using a different colour to highlight each topic. You can also order your material by writing key words in the margins, using code numbers or multiple asterisks and even by cutting and pasting all the relevant material and sticking it together. If you are writing directly on to a word-processor you can use number codes to group information, but it may be simpler to move blocks of text so that all similar material is grouped together. Although this may sound even more time consuming, it usually pays dividends in the long run as all your information, is conveniently ordered and you are less likely to miss bits out or to forget things if everything is grouped under separate topics. If you are looking at multiple markets for your work you can make a further grouping by using your own code for which material belongs to which market.

Storing tapes and notepads

When you have transcribed the tape to your satisfaction you need to keep it somewhere safe. Every tape you use should be labelled with the subject of the interview and the date and place. If you are intending to do a lot of interviews you will find it helpful to keep your interview tapes in a separate box from your jazz, classical or pop tapes and CDs. Never use the same interview tape twice and never record over what you have previously recorded. You should keep your tape or notepad of the interview for three years after the interview for libel reasons (see below). Another reason for keeping your tapes and notepad is that you may want to refer to them again at some point in the future, especially if you are writing another piece about the same subject.

Libel

I have included libel in the chapter on transcribing and writing up because it is at this stage where any libel will occur. The best advice about libel is that it is always better to avoid it in the first place and you can best prevent libel by being aware of the possibility of it happening whilst you are writing up. Your best defence against libel is always to work to professional standards with accuracy and fairness.

What is libel?

The laws of libel are complex and anyone who wishes to learn about them in detail should begin by consulting *McNae's Essential Law for Journalists* (see *Booklist*). Basically libel is a written false and/or defamatory statement (slander is libel which is spoken). A defamatory statement is one which damages someone's personal and/or professional reputation or exposes them to contempt and ridicule. Under current British law, if you write something which is both true and accurate, you may still be guilty of libel if the person concerned claims that the effect of what you have written has damaged either them or their reputation. Once you start to consider the laws of libel you can begin to wonder how anything ever gets written about anyone. Libel laws are heavily stacked against the writer and, whereas staff journalists can leave it to their employers to pick up the bill for a libel action, freelancers probably can't. For authors, most contracts contain a clause indemnifying the publishers against damages and costs for libel by the author. In practice the majority of people will not want to go through with suing over libel and the writer has certain defences against libel charges ('Fair comment' being the most common one) but as a beginner you should avoid any possibility of libel until you are fully informed of how libel works and how to defend yourself against it.

Avoiding libel

Your main safeguards against libel are the following:

- Make sure that what you write is accurate. Do not invent quotes or alter them in such a way as to significantly change what was said. This includes missing out significant parts of the quote, e.g. the Choirmaster's 'Of course, I have always taken great delight in choirboys' voices' written up as 'Of course, I have always taken great delight in choirboys' becomes libellous.

- Do not put in what was not said and do not make unwarranted assumptions about someone. An interesting example of how easily this can happen was when a young journalist interviewed a clergyman about his garden and wrote up in his piece words to the effect that: 'The Rev. loves nothing better than to spend time working alone in his garden'. The parson objected that, as a man of God, he loved nothing better than God and that it was potentially damaging to his reputation to say other than that. He won the case.

- Do not be tempted by juicy gossip that is slanderous. Even if the interviewee is saying it about someone else, you as the writer may be liable for libel.

- Be careful about identifying someone in a potentially incriminating position, no matter how innocent this really is, e.g. 'I met Harry Soames in the red-light district in Soho. He emerged from a shop rubbing his hands.'

- If in any doubt at all have your work checked – this could be by the person you are writing about (e.g. a doctor whose reputation may be damaged by your writing something inaccurate) or ask the publishers to have the manuscript read for potential libel. Most editors will spot a potential libel situation but you should not rely on this.

Libel incurs serious punishments both in fines and prison sentences. As a freelance writer you can protect yourself by considering very carefully the implications of what you are saying if you feel it is potentially libellous, keeping tapes which have not been recorded over (in this way you cannot be accused of doctoring the tape) and notepads which have not been altered for three years (this is because in 1985 the Administration of Justice Act introduced a three-year limitation period which states that legal proceedings for libel should begin within three years). A further protection is to familiarise yourself with libel law. Perhaps the best litmus test for libel is to ask yourself how you would feel if something similar were written about you.

Writing up

At the stage of transcribing your tape you have probably become acutely aware that there are no full stops and capital letters in the human voice. This is something you will need to deal with at the writing-up stage. The writing-up stage is the point at which you begin to put your work into its final form. The way in which you write up your interview material will be largely determined by the needs of the publication or audience for which you are writing. Some kinds of writing will consist entirely of quoting what the person said (an example of this is the 'Day in the life of. . .' feature, see below), others may need no quotes at all (biographers can interview many people whom they do not quote directly but whose interview provides supplementary information which helps them to form a broader picture of their subject) but most kinds of writing will require a mixture of both your own copy and the quotes of the interviewee.

Choosing what to use

You will almost certainly have more material in front of you from your transcription than you can possibly use. If you are writing an article of about 1000 words and have carried out a one-hour face-to-face interview, you will need to be selective about which material to include. You may reluctantly have to forgo using some useful material to keep within your word limit or, if you are doing several articles, may find that you reserve some information for another piece.

Precedents

The best way to determine how to write up your piece is by studying any available precedents. If you have researched your market thoroughly you should already have some idea of the preferred style (see also chapter 4). If you are writing for a specific slot in a magazine, e.g. a profile of the 'Mum of the week' for a woman's consumer magazine, you should carefully study several previous profiles to see what is the usual way of writing up the interview. If there is no precedent to go on, how you write up your piece is largely down to your own discretion but this should be informed by the following considerations:

- Who is the audience?
- What do they expect/want/need?
- What is the most appropriate style of writing?

House style

The style you use to write up your piece should be largely determined by the style of the kind of publication for which you are writing. For freelance journalists this is usually a relatively easy matter of scouring the relevant paper or magazine to get a feel for the kinds of acceptable writing for that publication. If there is no direct precedent, e.g. you are writing the first book ever about a particular subject, try to find a book in the same genre to get some idea – the style of books on local history differs considerably from books on humorous subjects; academic theses favour a particular style, whilst cookery books tend to favour another. Often simply reading through a similar piece will put you in the frame of mind for writing in that style. No two styles are the same and, as you continue to write your style will develop but a certain amount of imitation is a good way of starting out as a writer. Things to consider are:

- Sentence length.
- Vocabulary.
- Paragraph sizes.
- Uses of punctuation.
- Opening and closing paragraphs.

Editing the 'erms'

Human speech differs considerably from writing – in writing we tend to use better grammar, finish sentences, have fewer breaks and pauses and use capital letters, commas and full stops. Not so with the spoken word. Moreover human speech is full of redundancies of the 'erm', 'ah', 'mmm' variety, not to mention half finished sentences, sentences that have no particular use or meaning, over used phrases like 'I guess' and 'you know' and sentences that can run for ten minutes and more without a single break. If you are simply interviewing for information rather than for quotes, you will just need to extract the information you require but, if you need to get some good quotes, you will have to put what your interviewee has said into acceptable English without losing the flavour of what was said. Probably no interviewee wants to be represented on paper as incoherent, inarticulate or confused and in any case there would be little point in writing an interview if this was all that came across.

Extracting quotes

So long as you remain faithful to the actual essence and substance of what was said and do not add or subtract anything that alters it significantly, or use any uncharacteristic language, it is perfectly acceptable to edit what was said. Below are some examples of how this might be done.

EXAMPLE

The answer is circumlocutory

QUESTION: What advice would you give to an aspiring writer?

ANSWER: Well, I don't know really. I guess the first thing I would say is be persistent. It took me ten years to break in. I spent more time sweeping floors and working behind bars than I spent at my typewriter. Not that I minded it – especially the working behind bars bit because it gave me a lot of insight into how ordinary people live and what's on their minds and things like that. Being around all that alcohol wasn't too bad either. So I suppose that's another thing – writers should go out and see a bit of life first, not like these academic people who don't know a saloon bar from a lounge. . .

In this example there is potential material for writing about several aspects of the interviewee (his earlier life, his opinion on academia and possible leanings towards alcoholism) but you want to glean what advice he would give to aspiring writers so you may quote him: 'The first thing is be persistent – it took me ten years to break in and all writer's should go out and see a bit of life first.'

EXAMPLE

The answer contains a number of self-contradictions

QUESTION: When did you buy your first Rolls-Royce?

ANSWER: Ooh that would be. . . now let me see. It was 1987, the year my sister – no hang on a minute, it was before that. Or was it? I know it was the summer of 1986, the year I had my first hit single – that was 'Motorway Dreams'. Do you remember that one?

In this example the above quote may simply yield the following information: 'I bought my first Rolls Royce in 1986, the same year that 'Motorway Dreams ' became a chart topper'. Although this answer is so confused that it might be better to use a paraphrase.

EXAMPLE

The answer is evasive

QUESTION: So why did you marry a man sixty years older than yourself?

ANSWER: Well, I guess I married for a lot of reasons – it's not easy to put my finger on it but I guess Terry and I were, well, let me put it like this when we first met there was something there that I can't explain I guess you could call it a meeting of minds or something I don't think I can quantify it exactly but let's just say there was something between us'

In this example you could write it up as: 'She hesitates to say exactly what she and Terry Conlon have in common but says it was "a meeting of minds from the start" and that "There was just something between us".'

If you were writing for a slightly risqué market you might like to query exactly what it is that's between them.

Paraphrasing

Sometimes you may find it easier to paraphrase what someone has said rather than try to make a quote out of it. It is perfectly reasonable to alternate between quotes and paraphrases (except in some kinds of writing such as 'A Day in the life of. . .' – see below where a particular format is required), but again your paraphrases should not make any significant alterations to the essence of what was said.

EXAMPLE

QUESTION: What was the most memorable event of your time as an evacuee in the war?

ANSWER: Well, I suppose what I liked best about it was being in the countryside err, you know it was really lovely waking up to the sound of the cows mooing our George used to say it was like something out of a book you know one of them books they used to have written by that children's writer I forget her name about children growing up on a farm. I always used to think that the sound of the cows in the fields in the morning was one of the most peaceful sounds in the world even though you could sometimes hear the fighters going overhead. Well I suppose that's what I liked best really.

In this example you want to extract the significant information. The write-up of this could be: 'She remembers with greatest affection the sound of the cows lowing in the morning, an affection that was not diminished by the occasional noise of the fighter planes overhead.' If you wanted a direct quote it might be: 'I always used to think that the sound of cows in the fields in the morning was one of the most peaceful sounds in the world.'

Retaining the flavour

Do not think that you have to turn what everyone says into bland middle-of-the-road English. Character and circumstances are often revealed through the way someone speaks. In some cases it may add considerably to your piece if you try to retain the flavour of the accent or dialect in your writing. If you are writing an oral history of your village, you will make your writing richer and more authentic if your retain dialect words and regional accents as far as possible. If need be, you can explain any totally obscure words through footnotes. However, do not attempt to render an accent in printed words unless you can do it well and do not make your interviewee sound like a bumpkin. Interviewing children can often provide funny and moving copy simply by rendering accurately what they are saying.

Don't let them look stupid

Some interviewees will do most of the work for you if they are articulate, speak grammatically and finish what they have started saying. Such people are, however, a minority. Sports personalities (particularly footballers and football commentators) are often the subject of ridicule for the way they speak and the content of what they say. It is not a good idea to try to make your interviewees look stupid or uneducated on paper – apart from anything else it will probably say more about you than them. Malapropisms, dropped aitches, bad grammar and obvious contradictions ('It was in the penultimate game that he really came into his own. The two that followed were a bit of a let down.') should not be kept unless they serve a specific purpose (this does not include ridicule at your interviewee's expense). People can often make mistakes in an interview situation just because they are nervous.

Preserving anonymity

As said in chapter 9, *In the event of. . .* some interviewees may not wish to be directly identified with the piece you are writing. If you have come to an agreement to keep the person's identity secret, you will probably need to inform your editor who should understand why this is so and may in fact have already suggested to you that certain persons' identities are not revealed. You would not normally even have to disclose the interviewee's true identity to the editor. You should, however, state in your piece or article that you are not using real names. You can do this by either writing in brackets after the name, e.g. 'John (not his real name)' or by adding a footnote at the end to the effect that 'Names have been changed to protect interviewees' privacy'.

Forms of writing up

Day in the life of. . .

This is the kind of piece which is often written as if the interviewees were writing it themselves because everything is said in the first person with no interjections from the interviewer. It is fairly common in weekend magazines. Sometimes the interview may actually have been written by the interviewees but usually they have been asked a number of questions to provide comprehensive information about a typical day and these have been carefully edited by the interviewer.

EXAMPLE

'A Day in the life. . .' article may begin: 'My day begins when the dog leaps on the bed and licks my face. My husband gets jealous but it's a case of love me, love my dog.'

Questions which might have been asked to produce this information are:

QUESTION: When does your day start?

ANSWER: Usually when Bonzo (that's my rotweiler) jumps all over the bed asking to be let out for a pee. He always comes to me first and gives me a huge slobbering kiss on the cheek.

QUESTION: Doesn't your husband gets jealous?

ANSWER: Oh yeah, but he has to lump it. It's a case of love me, love my dog as they say.

In this kind of interview the interviewer's presence is largely hidden and has no evident bearing on the contents of the interview. The skill is in trying to make a number of possibly disconnected answers combine to sound as if the person is continuously describing a day rather than stopping to answer questions. This kind of write-up should sound as if it is flowing naturally. The interviewer has to be fairly selective about what information to use, bearing in mind both the intended audience and the number of words at his/her disposal.

Question-and-answer format

This is a piece of writing where there may be an introduction and possibly a conclusion but the bulk of the writing consists of the actual questions and answers. Whilst the answers may be edited to make them sound more coherent, the order in which they were asked is probably kept.

EXAMPLE:

Jane Brain is interviewing Selina Donna about how she managed to find work in France as one of several case histories for a 'How to' book on living and working in France:

JB: How easy was it to find work in France?

SB: I found it relatively easy. I have a degree in modern languages and a post-graduate diploma in teaching. I think the fact that I knew the language and had a professional qualification helped me considerably.

JB: How did you go about looking for work?

SB: At first I tried looking in the English newspapers such as the *Guardian* and the *Times Educational Supplement* but there were no jobs in Brittany which was the area where I specifically wanted to work because my partner lives there. In the end I went over to France and telephoned a few language schools directly. I got a very good response from all of them and three of them offered me work there and then.

In many ways these are the simplest kinds of interviews. Case histories, questionnaires and straight, factual articles often draw on this format.

Quotes and comments

Many articles consist of a number of quotes (and or paraphrases) inter-spersed with your own observations, descriptions or comments. Usually the input of the interviewee should outweigh that of the interviewer - after all it is the interviewee that is the subject of interest. In this kind of writing, particularly for profiles, the interviewer should provide the links and coherence between what is said. These kind of articles have the advantage of almost literally writing themselves as they usually contain a large number of quotes which can fill out quite a lot of copy.

EXAMPLE from a profile article for a business men's magazine:

Some people might find living in Chelsea and working in Hong Kong a commuting nightmare but David White, managing director of White and White plc, doesn't think so: 'I love the thrill of just getting on a plane and taking off to the other side of the world,' he says. 'I'm always glad to arrive in Hong Kong and equally glad to get back home in London.'

Speaking at his Chelsea pad, White relaxes with a glass of malt whisky and his dog Fido, a cairn terrier. His wife, the model Linda Cambron, is expected later. He looks happy and relaxed despite a recent jet hop from Hong Kong. But doesn't all this commuting place a strain on his social life, I wonder?

'Not really. I socialise where I work and I like to stay at home when I'm at home. . .'

In this example the comments of the interviewer add to the overall picture of the subject – what he looks like, who his wife is, what whisky he drinks, etc.

General opinion

There may be occasions when there is no need to mention or quote your interviewee at all in your writing. If you have interviewed a number of people on a particular subject, you may just want to record the overall impression, for example, a number of old school colleagues discussing a famous old pupil for a biographical account.

EXAMPLE

Fellow pupils recall that Schwarzman was a loner who preferred his own company to that of other boys. He was noted for spending large amounts of time alone in the library when he could have been out participating in the more usual schoolboy pursuits of cricket, rugby and smoking behind the garden shed.

Specialist opinion

If you have sought expert information, for instance, for a medical piece, from several sources, you can similarly give the overall findings: 'Medical experts are sceptical about the claims of the new wonder drug for AIDS and would like to see more trials before the drug is launched on to the market next year.'

If an individual has given you advice it is polite to acknowledge this: 'Dr Michael Sargents of University College Hospital, Berfordshire, expressed reservations about the new so-called wonder drug and said that there was a need for more trials.'

If you are recording information given to you by a press officer it is usual to write up: 'A spokeswoman for the British Medical Association. . .', etc., but if the information is fairly commonplace it may not be necessary to involve your source at all.

EXAMPLE

'A source at the Icelandic Embassy in London said that the population of Iceland is just over a quarter of a million. They added that the birth rate is rising annually by one and a quarter per cent.'
would probably sound better as:

'With a population of just over a quarter of a million and an annual population growth of one and a quarter per cent, Iceland. . .'

When writing it is important that you make yourself sound informed or at least as if you have done some research. Apart from anything else, the information about Iceland can probably be found in the library. As a general rule only quote the experts when you are presenting information that you could not have got yourself, when it gains credibility by being attributed to a particular source or is said in a particularly quotable way.

The interviewee is absent

In some kinds of writing, particularly academic theses, you may not consider it necessary to mention the contents of an interview at all. In this case you can either use footnotes to indicate where your information came from or acknowledge the help given to you in the introduction. For more on acknowledgements see the next chapter.

You and the interview

How much you choose to reveal of yourself when writing up the interview is a matter for your discretion. Factual pieces of writing are not generally enhanced by the presence of the writer in the piece and in more academic and formal pieces the presence of the writer is almost entirely superfluous. Newcomers to writing and interviewing have a tendency to overstate the obvious. Writing something like: 'Armed with my tape recorder and feeling nervous I set out to interview. . .' both sounds and is amateurish. It is also saying more about you than your subject and you, after all, are not the main point of the interview. Unless you are relevant in some way, there is no need to mention yourself at all. Examples of where interviewers could talk about themselves are if they had a particular effect on the interviewee and vice versa.

EXAMPLE

[Interviewee speaking] 'Of course, Samuel Beckett was in a different league to James Joyce. Different kettle of fish altogether. don't you think?'

I nod dimly. Henry Richards has a way of making you recognise your ignorance, whilst making the charming assumption that you are as erudite as he is.

EXAMPLE

Walking up the garden path with a man whose writing contains more dismembered bodies than membered ones, I was surprised to see him stoop to pick up a caterpillar from under his tread. . .

If you decide to include yourself do not sound over-awed – it is amateurish – even if you were, e.g. 'I sat on the edge of the chair and wondered which of the ten pieces of cutlery before me I should use first.' Some interviewers are personalities in their own right and may have a readership which is as interested in their exploits as it is in those of the interviewee. Do not start off by assuming that anyone is interested in you unless you can include yourself in a way that is particularly well written or entertaining.

I asked/He said

Avoid over use of phrases like 'he said/replied/answered. . .' and 'I asked/wondered/enquired. . .' These rapidly start to sound rather tedious and there are many alternative ways of indicating that your interviewee is speaking or answering a question. If you are not sure of any alternatives, try looking at the way other writers have got round the 'I asked/he said' problem. You do not always have to say what your question was in the actual written piece (see 'Day in the Life of. . .' for an example) and, unless you are adding a personal comment, you do not need to draw attention to the fact that this is an interview at all; for example, 'I asked Mr Bigbucks what he thinks the prospects for his business are in the next six months. "Excellent," he said and added "We are looking forward to a bumper year".' This could be written as: 'Bigbucks is looking forward to a bumper year and described business prospects for the next six months as "Excellent".'

12
AFTERWARDS

When your interview is over and you have written up your piece, there are a few odds and ends to tie together before sending off your work for publication. This is the final stage of the interviewing process and the chapter concludes with a look ahead to future interviews.

The thank-you letter

You may feel that if someone has given you a particularly good interview or has provided a lot of time and effort to help you that you would like to extend a thank you above and beyond the one that you hopefully gave at your last meeting. If this is the case, sending a card is perfectly reasonable. People like to be told that they have been helpful and you may also be paving the way for further interviews, as well as smoothing the path for anyone else who wants to come along and interview them.

Forwarding copy for checking

As explained in chapter 9, *In the event of. . .,* you would not normally forward your piece for an interviewee to check unless it was important that the contents were approved by an expert before being published. Always remember to retain a copy for yourself when you send off work to be checked. If you are sending the work by fax you will keep the original but, if not and you are working on a word-processor, take a copy on a floppy disk. Those using a typewriter should take either a carbon copy or a photocopy. If your interviewee is an important expert, remember that boffins have a reputation for absent-mindedness and, whether this is true or not, you do not want to put the theory to the test by using the only copy of your masterpiece. Another thing to remember about boffins is that they are usually busy and may not give your piece of work priority. As you may be coming up to a deadline, you should enclose with your piece of work a letter explaining that your manuscript must reach the editor by a certain date (you can always bring the date forward to stress the urgency). Tell your interviewees that you would like it to be returned to you by a given date at the latest when you will submit it and that, if you have not heard back by then, you will assume that the piece meets with their approval. This way you have given them fair warning. Alternatively you can say that you have retained a copy and will ring them up in a few days time to see if anything needs changing. The latter course is probably the safer one. If you want the work returned, enclose an SAE. Remember that you are asking them only to check for potential inaccuracies. It is not their job to comment on your writing style or to suggest that you do parts of it differently or to say that they don't like the font of your printer. If they do comment on things like this, listen dispassionately but don't feel that you should undertake to change anything unless it makes sense to you to do so.

Let your editor know that the manuscript has been checked when you finally submit it for publication – you will earn brownie points for having been so professional.

Marketing the work

A final polish

When you have written up your piece let it 'stand' for a few days. This is because it is easy to become so engrossed in your writing that you are unable to assess it objectively. You need to come back to your work again in the cold light of day with a clear and fresh mind. See how it strikes you then – this is probably how it will strike the editor and ultimately the reader when they come to read it. For journalists working to a deadline there may be a time limit in which to do this but for other kinds of writing such as books and theses there will usually be a lengthy polishing and revision period at the end of the first draft.

Presentation

Presentation is nearly as important as content when approaching an editor. The way you present your work is the first impression you make. Different publishers have different requirements and, if your project is particularly large – a book, for example – you should be made aware of this when you get the contract. Increasingly there has been a move away from hard copy (i.e. the printed page) to the use of computer disks but most publishers still want both and you should make sure that your work is properly presented on paper, even if you are enclosing a disk with the hard copy. The majority of magazines and newspapers still use hard copy. There are many books available explaining how to present manuscripts for publishers and an entire exposition is beyond the scope of this book but below is a basic run down of some of the main requirements:

- Paper should be A4 size and should be of good strength and thickness.
- Type on one side of the page only with sufficient margins (about 4cm is usually sufficient) around the entire text.
- The manuscript (including bibliography and footnotes) should be double spaced in black ink.
- Number each page.
- Make sure your work has a title and include your name, address and telephone number with your piece either on a covering page or on the first page.

Needless to say manuscripts which look as if they have been used as coffee mats do not create a very good impression. When sending your manuscripts use envelopes that will take A4 paper unfolded. Enclose an SAE if you want it to be returned and, if you are worried about its safe arrival send it recorded delivery. Always keep a copy of your work for yourself.

If you have a commission (mainly journalists)

If you have been given a written or verbal commission for your work you should forward it as soon as you have written and checked it to your satisfaction. It is very easy to procrastinate once you have written the piece but you should avoid dithering over sending it off for three good reasons:

- The sooner it is sent off the sooner it is ready for publication.
- The sooner it is published the sooner you get paid.
- You gain brownie points with an editor if you deliver a piece in good time.

Enclose a covering note with your piece reminding the editor of the telephone conversation or written communication you had about the piece. Specifically mention that it has been commissioned so that editors cannot go back on their word.

If you have had a maybe

If editors have expressed interest in your piece but have not made a specific commission (either because you are an unknown and they do not want to take any risks or because they are not entirely sure of the suitability of the piece for the publication) send it off with a covering note reminding them of any previous communication about it. Whilst editors are not obliged to accept your piece, the fact that they have shown interest is a good indicator that they will want to publish it, providing that your piece is suitable for the publication.

On spec

If you have done your interview before finding a market for your work – either because you have just grasped a vital opportunity to interview someone and not had time to find a market or because you felt it would be preferable to do the interview first and find a publication second – the procedure is the same as that outlined in chapter 4, *Finding a market*. You can either ring editors and ask whether they would be interested in your piece or send it directly to the publication with a covering note saying what the piece is about, why you think it is suitable for that publication and anything relevant about yourself and your background that will help sell your piece to the editor.

Multiple marketing of interviews

If you want to make money from writing articles you need to use your time and resources effectively. The best way of doing this with interviews is to sell as many articles as possible on the one subject. The main consideration when writing several pieces about the same subject is that you should not write two similar pieces for rival publications – for instance, by writing two pieces on a celebrity's exercise workout for two health and fitness magazines. You should also avoid using the same quotes or ideas and above all do not repeat your own writing. When you are doing multiple marketing, each piece you write should be entirely separate from the others and should have a different angle.

Perhaps the ultimate way to remarket your interviews is to turn them into a biography. This is also another reason for keeping hold of the information you have gathered and for trying to part with your interviewee on good terms.

Sending photos

If you have taken photographs of your interviewee you will need to forward them to the editor. Some book contracts state that all illustrations, maps, notes, etc., should be forwarded with the manuscript but, in the case of magazine articles which may be published several months hence, it often makes more sense to hold on to your photos until the editor is ready. This is because editorial offices are often busy and untidy places where things can go astray very easily. Whilst it is relatively easy to forward another copy of a manuscript (assuming that you have kept one), loss of photographs means more time and expense in getting new photos printed and, as many editors make a disclaimer that they cannot accept responsibility for loss of or damage to your manuscript and photos whilst they are in their care, the expense will fall to you. It is therefore a matter of self-protection to minimise the chances of this happening. When you send off your manuscript to a magazine or newspaper editor, explain in your covering note that you have got the photos and will forward them when the editor is ready. An alternative is to send the editor a contact sheet which will contain all the photos on your roll of film. Editors can then choose which photo(s) they like best – for more on this talk to the people in your local camera shop who will be able to advise you. When you send photos, put them in a strong envelope with a hard back. Always send them recorded delivery. Unlike manuscripts, photos always remain your copyright and should be returned to you when they have been used.

You can further prevent loss of photos by writing your name and address on self-adhesive labels and sticking one on the back of every picture (you can also do this by using a rubber stamp with your details). Do not write directly on the back of photos as this may mark them. If you are providing captions for your photos attach these to the back in a similar way. Transparencies can be posted in special storage wallets available from most camera shops. Label the wallet and include a list of captions with the appropriate transparency number on a separate piece of paper.

Acknowledgments

Most interviewees appreciate being appreciated and, as they have probably given freely of their time, energy and expertise, it is only good manners to acknowledge this help where possible. Often you can do this by identifying them as the source of a particular piece of information, e.g. 'Dr Phillip Saunders, medical director of the Biochemistry Research Unit of the Berfordshire Royal hospital, expressed scepticism about. . .' It is not always possible to identify someone directly but if you are writing a book there will usually be a space at the front for acknowledgments. Sometimes acknowledgements are incorporated into the preface where the author makes personal comments about how and why the book came into being and thanks all those who helped in the making of it – classically this is where male authors thank their wives and secretaries for doing the typing. Often acknowledgements form a list preceded by something like 'special thanks to the following whose help has been invaluable in the writing of this book. . .' If there are a great many people to acknowledge (as is sometimes the case with biographies), a separate page for acknowledgments may be used. You may wish to single out people who have been particularly helpful, e.g. 'Special thanks to John Smith of the Berfordshire Museum who helped me above and beyond the call of duty and was tireless in answering my irritating questions. . .', etc. If you are unsure of an appropriate wording look at the 'prelims' (initial pages before a book's main text) of a similar publication to see how it has been done.

Complimentary copies of books
It is common practice for book publishers to forward a number of presentation copies to the author of the work on publication. Where you feel it is appropriate, you could present copies to people who have been particularly helpful. Alternatively, let them know when the book will be published and they will probably go out and buy one which will boost your royalties. Many people are deeply flattered and excited to see their names in a book and may be far more grateful to you than you are to them.

Complimentary copies of articles
People who have been interviewed sometimes ask to be forwarded a copy of the magazine or paper when your article comes out. This raises certain issues. You may yourself not be forwarded a copy of the publication and, if you are, you will almost certainly not be sent more than one. If you are sent a copy you will probably want to keep it for yourself to put in your scrapbook or file of published articles. In such cases you could send a photocopy of the relevant articles but you can preempt this to some extent by telling the interviewees when they can expect to see the article – if, that is, you know yourself. Alternatively you could say that you are not quite sure but that it will probably be at a certain period. Finally, you could always say that it is not common practice to forward copies but you will mention it to the editor. The chances are they will probably be only too eager to go out and buy ten copies to show their friends if they are not used to seeing their name in print.

From here
Your first few interviews are often both the most difficult and the most exciting ones. If you are intending to go on to interview regularly as part of your writing and researching career you will doubtless want to build on your skills and techniques. Whilst the only way to become a good interviewer is to go out and interview, you can gain valuable insights into good interviewing techniques by reading the interviews in newspapers, magazines and books. Begin to read with a more critical eye, look at how

successful journalists and writers have tackled interviews, make a mental or actual note of anything you think is particularly successful or that you think doesn't work. Turn reading the papers in bed on Sunday morning into a valuable exercise in criticism. See how quotes are written up and paraphrased and try to work out what particular question elicited a particular response. To find out more about interviews in action, watch how television interviewers tackle their subjects and listen to radio interviews to see what they can teach you.

Practise in your own work too – experiment with ways of writing up interviews and become your own editor. Try reading your work as if it belonged to someone else or get an honest but constructive friend to criticise your work for you. Most important of all, remember that your best learning ground will be out in the real world doing as many kinds of interviews as you can.

Good Luck!

BOOK LIST

Centres and Bureaux: a Directory of Effort, Information and Expertise (CBD Research Ltd)

Charities Digest (Family Welfare Association)

Councils, Committees and Boards: Handbook of Advisory, Consultative, Executive and Similar Bodies in British Public Life (CBD Research Ltd)

Current British Directories (CBD Research Ltd)

Dod's Parliamentary Companion (Dod's Parliamentary Companion)

Major Companies Guide (Directory of Social Change)

McNae's Essential Law for Journalists by Tom Welsh and Walter Greenwood (Butterworths, 13th edition)

Reminiscence Work with Old People by Clare Gillies and Anne James (Chapman & Hall)

Research for Writers by Ann Hoffmann (A & C Black)

The Voluntary Agencies Directory (NCVO Publications)

Who's Who (A & C Black)

The Writer's Handbook by Barry Turner (Macmillan)

Trade Associations and Professional Bodies of the United Kingdom (Gale Research Inc.)

Whitiker's Almanack (Whitaker)

Writers' & Artists' Yearbook (A & C Black)

INDEX

NOTES